VENTURE
EVERYWHERE

VENTURE EVERYWHERE

{ **Travel, Entrepreneurship and a Roadmap for Life** }

JENNY FIELDING

Post Hill
PRESS

A POST HILL PRESS BOOK
ISBN: 979-8-88845-731-3
ISBN (eBook): 979-8-88845-732-0

Venture Everywhere:
Travel, Entrepreneurship, and a Roadmap for Life
© 2025 by Jenny Fielding
All Rights Reserved

Cover design by Lynn Rawden

Post Hill Press
New York • Nashville
posthillpress.com

Published in the United States of America
1 2 3 4 5 6 7 8 9 10

For founders, EVERYWHERE

TABLE OF CONTENTS

INTRODUCTION

My twin passions for entrepreneurship and travel sprouted and became entwined at my grandparents' house in Flatbush, Brooklyn, when I was a little kid.

My parents dropped me off there every weekend; I loved stepping into their space, which was a blend of bold patterns and knickknacks, stuffed full of large ornate pieces of furniture that would have fit in well at Versailles and a different pattern of 3D wallpaper in every room.

My grandpa Al owned fruit stores all over Brooklyn and, for the majority of his adult life, woke up at 4:00 a.m., seven days a week and visited all of the stores, taking precise inventory, overseeing deliveries, and gracefully managing each store's relationship with the "roughnecks" (in other words, the mafia—fruit stores create a lot of garbage!) through a combination of charisma and a pair of Dobermanns.

I think I get a lot of my business acumen—not to mention self-possession—from him.

By the time he sold all the stores and retired, he had plenty of time to spend with me, most typically turning their coffee table into a blackjack table, where we would play cards and shoot craps using solid gold dice.

He had never gone to college himself, but my grandpa was, in many ways, ahead of his time. He believed that modern women needed to be independent, financially and otherwise, and naturally concluded that winning at cards was the best way to achieve that goal. So, by the age of six, I was on my way.

He also wore all kinds of gold jewelry, gold rings, and a neck full of gold chains.

When my grandma passed away, I spotted this gaudy but distinct diamond-and-ruby pink-gold ring in her jewelry box, decided that it was going to be my new look, and started wearing it.

One day I saw my mom, showed her my hand, and said, "Mom, doesn't it make you happy that I wear grandma's ring every day?"

My mother smiled and said, "Yes honey, it makes me happy—but that's not grandma's ring. It's grandpa's."

I love carrying him with me, and I still put that ring on sometimes when the mood strikes.

For her part, my grandma was in a category all her own. Her name was Pearl London, and she had bright orange hair, wore hot-pink, bejeweled sweatsuits, and was the quintessential explorer, endlessly curious about everything in the world. She was a frequent cruiser to Cuba, a high-rolling gambler in Vegas, and she thought trains were the most romantic way to travel to and through far-flung places.

One evening when we were playing gin rummy (no need to worry about mundane things like homework in my grandparents' house when we could stay up extra late watching *Love Boat* and *Fantasy Island* reruns instead, much to my more straight-laced parents' consternation), I heard my grandma on the phone telling the person on the other end about a month-long European trip she was taking soon.

Right then, at the age of nine, I felt the first real pull of adventure. I *knew* I needed to go on that trip.

"Grandma," I said, halting the cartwheels I'd been practicing down their long hallway and coming to stop in front of her when she came back into the room. "Please take me with you on your trip."

My grandma sat down like a queen (or maybe more like a magic genie) on her oversized brocade chair, eyeing me with a mix of amusement and thoughtfulness, her halo of red hair lit up and her jeweled hands and wrists twinkling from the light pouring in the bay window in the living room.

Convincing her was easy. Convincing my parents was more challenging, as they didn't *exactly* think my freewheeling grandmother was the best influence for me.

But somehow, she did it, and a few weeks later, we were off.

"Are you ready for an adventure, darling?" she asked as we boarded the first of many transcontinental trains we'd be taking through several European countries for the next month.

"I'm ready, Grandma," I told her confidently.

Every time we landed in a new city, she'd pass me a guidebook and ask, "What are we going to do and see today?"

Grandma was truly up for anything, sweeping into rooms and cities alike, ready for any new discovery around the corner. It was contagious.

And what I loved about—and learned from—my grandma was that she never tried to mold me into something I wasn't or something *she* wanted me to be. She was the epitome of open-minded, and I had no idea how much of an impact that would have on my entire personal and professional trajectory until much, much later.

At the time, I was on a salami kick (I literally wanted to eat it at every meal), and instead of encouraging me to eat eggs to start the day or chicken for dinner, we sampled cured meat in Madrid, and I ate charcuterie for breakfast in Munich.

We strolled through Paris, people-watched in *terrasses*, and met up with her friends, with whom I interacted as if they were contemporaries, even though they had a solid seven decades on me. In Amsterdam, I showed Grandma how to ride a bike without gears, and we cruised up and down the canals with her multitude of bracelets and necklaces tinkling and her hot-pink velour sweatpants blazing like a beacon (you could literally see them a mile away) with huge grins on both of our faces. Hamburg introduced me to distant relatives who didn't speak much English but who embraced us with open arms (and happily fed me more salami!).

When we'd arrive at a new hotel, she'd say, "Honey, here's your key," adding, "That way, you can explore the hotel on your own." As an only child and a New York City kid, I was very independent, mature, and self-sufficient, so this might be a little weird by today's standards, but it wasn't at all then, for me.

Down in the hotel restaurant, I'd nibble at whatever snacks were placed out for us, and Grandma would have a couple of martinis, then go up to our room for a nap. I'd wander through the halls, absorbing the sights, smells, and sounds of so many different cultures and languages under one roof—ones I didn't understand. Yet.

I was wide-eyed with wonder, but at the same time, I felt at home; those hotel keys opened doors that would change my life in magical ways.

The travel spark was ignited in me like a firework after my trip with my grandma, but instead of convincing my parents to let me go to boarding school in Switzerland to start my journey as a global citizen in earnest (and boy, did I try), I was unceremoniously escorted back into my old life and onto a more traditional path.

A little later, I was back at my grandparents' for the weekend and rummaging around their basement when I came across a massive and well-loved world atlas. While the cover was tattered and starting to yellow, the inside was pristine with brightly colored, waxed-page illustrations and maps. I opened it and devoured every page, right there among the storage boxes and dust, smoothing my hand over the pages reverently.

I carried that atlas with me everywhere, and at school, I started The Secret Explorers Club—an informal gathering of other nerdy kids who also happened to love my atlas. We would meet up at lunch to plan world expeditions, despite the fact that no one was really going anywhere, except perhaps, eventually, down to Wall Street or up to Bronxville.

⇦⇨

Fast forward to the years after law school. By then, I'd traveled some more and experienced some of the world, lived in Mexico for a year (more on that later), and found myself back in New York, working for J.P. Morgan but dating a guy who lived in Germany.

That's when the second spark ignited (and not just of the romantic kind).

After my third or fourth monthly cell phone bill topping $1,000, I realized that we (the millions of people across the US making direct international calls) had a problem. I decided to fix it by leaving the comfort of the corporate world to become a technology entrepreneur. After founding two mobile software companies and breaking up with my German boyfriend (sorry, Johann!), I eventually turned to the "dark" side and became a venture capitalist.

But that pivot shone a light on my purpose: combining my abiding passions for travel and entrepreneurship and using them to address some of the problems and inefficiencies I saw around me while creating opportunities to improve the world.

That meant investing in and working with the founders building companies far from the glow of Silicon Valley.

꩜

My grandmother was probably the earliest embodiment for me of an Everywhere Mindset, and that idea kept compounding throughout my personal and professional life until it became a drumbeat too loud to ignore.

The year I started my first company (2007), I talked to a friend who'd just returned from a trip to the Philippines. He told me money could be wired to a Philippine account, and the recipient could pick up the cash at their local McDonalds while paying for a Big Mac. My mind was blown; in those days, most people in the US didn't even use online banking, never mind mobile banking.

In that, I saw a future that didn't exist (at least here in America), and I had to be part of it. Since then, I've dedicated my professional life and passion to both building and investing in startups and have never looked back.

I've always been interested in international founders—not necessarily household names in the US but people who are prominent in their geographies and communities—which has informed the global thesis of my venture capital fund, Everywhere Ventures.

"Globalization" is usually thought of in terms of economics and politics, but *Venture Everywhere: Travel, Entrepreneurship, and a Roadmap for Life* will demonstrate that it's so much bigger than that.

With all of the founders I've met in my fifteen-plus years as a founder and investor, as well as the ones I interviewed for *Venture Everywhere*, patterns emerged among the wildly different personalities and circumstances I came across. Through them, I developed a global set of principles and perspectives called the "Everywhere Mindset," which forms a roadmap for success in both business and life. It includes qualities such as being ELASTIC, having CONVICTION, being KINETIC, having MOXIE, thinking MACRO, and being SYSTEMATIC. Most surprising to me is that the same characteristic might manifest differently from one person to the next, but seen in context, the unique stories paint a very similar big picture.

I'll show how the Everywhere Mindset is about social and cultural change and development; we *all* need to become global citizens to get ahead in work and life, and entrepreneurs are paving the way for this new thinking.

Each chapter of *Venture Everywhere* lands in a particular geographical area and covers my experiences and stories in that place, both personal and professional (and at times, comical). I also describe the business and startup culture there, sharing insights and context.

The individual chapters will also have a companion founder profile—related in some way to the geographical area I explore in the core of the chapter. Each profile will be underpinned by one of the six characteristics of the Everywhere Mindset and demonstrate how the founder used it to be successful in their work, as well as how that trait can be cultivated and nurtured more broadly.

This isn't a typical business book with formal lessons, but whether you're an entrepreneur, investor, career-switcher, or travel enthusiast, you'll benefit from the concepts within.

The founders I interview originate in what many consider far-flung places—ranging from Brazil to Barcelona, Saudi Arabia to the Philippines, and everywhere in between. Learning about and (often) investing in and working with these inspirational people has revealed to me the secret they've unlocked about how the world works…and that's having an Everywhere Mindset.

Through that concept, *Venture Everywhere* will help people develop business, life, and interpersonal skills, all wrapped up in my entertaining travelog, highlighting the aspects of the cultures and places I find truly fascinating.

Ultimately, it's not about simply sending your kids to Mandarin class or memorizing capital cities on a map; it's about having empathy and awareness for other cultures and realizing the world is increasingly more interconnected. At almost any company or in any role, people will have inter-cultural experiences through team members, leaders, and customers, and now, with the rise of distributed teams, every company is relying on global talent. Showing openness and being comfortable working in these diverse (and context-switching) environments is a necessary skill that bestows a competitive edge in today's business environment.

More than anything, though, *Venture Everywhere* is a "permission slip" for the person who wants to live, travel, build, and experience all life has to offer. You don't have to be born in Silicon Valley to be a great entrepreneur, and you don't need what you might think you need to build a career or business, grow or evolve in your career, or stay relevant. You don't have to play by the rules and live in one place. Success doesn't mean twenty years at a huge corporation and a gold watch upon retirement; it means charting your own path.

I'm offering my readers the inspiration—and the liberation—to become global citizens and creators, free from bygone societal expectations and norms. For those of us in the know, it's a new playbook for how to live.

CHAPTER 1

MEXICO

My senior year in college, not knowing what I wanted to do with my life, I applied to law school. But when it came time to enroll, I got cold feet and decided to defer and take a gap year in Mexico. I worked my ass off saving up and living at home, working nights and weekends at a popular French restaurant in the West Village (an interesting choice considering I was heading to a Spanish-speaking country) and as a production assistant on movies during the day. I don't think I slept for six months straight, but I saved enough to live in Mexico for the following eight months.

I hopped on a plane and headed down there, not knowing anyone but with a dream of apprenticing with a renowned sculptor in San Miguel de Allende (SMA as it is referred to locally)—a small artsy town a few hours north of Mexico City. Despite majoring in history and political science in college, I had this artistic side to me and a right brain that craved creativity, while knowing full well my professional destiny as a lawyer was going to look much different...or so I thought!

Upon arriving in SMA, I settled into a cute hotel and then set out to find a more permanent place to live. This being pre-Facebook and WhatsApp, I spent the first week holding court at the local cafe and language-learning center near El Jardin (also called the Zócalo, a leafy central square found in many Mexican towns), which was run by an awesome couple; she was from Boston, and he was from Mexico City, and they had met when he was an exchange student in the US.

They'd decided to create a fun "alternative" life for themselves (obviously anchored in the Everywhere Mindset) where they worked together, so they set up the cafe in town, then the language school. It was an informal meeting spot and definitely the place to make new friends, find a roommate, and eat mind-blowing, freshly-baked banana bread.

One day, a woman with bright-orange lipstick and flowing robes burst into the cafe, immediately reminding me of Grandma Pearl with her larger-than-life presence and trail of animals (not to mention drama, which I would learn about later) following close behind her.

Her name was Marie. She was originally from the UK and had followed her Mexican lover to San Miguel in the early 1980s. When they eventually broke up, she "took to her bed" (as she dramatically described to me later) and didn't come out of the house for five years—at least according to local town folklore. When Marie finally emerged, she had embraced a new spiritual life, collected half a dozen cats, and started hosting meditation and chanting classes in the courtyard of her home.

She also rented a free-standing casita at the top of her house to make some extra pesos, and she'd come to the art cafe that day to post about a vacancy.

It felt like kismet, and, wide open to new experiences, I followed her back to the house to check out the casita. The rent was super reasonable, so I should not have been surprised to learn that, in order to access the stairs to the casita, one needed to navigate through floor pillows, stacking meditation rugs and blankets, plus whatever chanting and gatherings were happening in the courtyard.

But once on the roof, the casita was among the most beautiful, almost mystical, spots in all of town, with full views of the cathedral in El Jardin as well as the bull ring across the street. I immediately fell in love and felt so lucky to have stumbled into it.

Living in a small town in Mexico was an eye-opener after coming from New York City where everyone seems to have an intense job in a big office building with a "live-to-work" attitude. In SMA, people worked hard—they were self-motivated and resourceful, and most of them had multiple jobs and side hustles—but they also really seemed to relax and enjoy life too. There were so many business owners—restaurant and bakery proprietors, exporters of crafts, my friends who ran the cafe and language school—which painted it with a very entrepreneurial (and inspiring) brush from my vantage point.

Along with Pepe, the mangy stray dog that slept under our doorstep, I collected a menagerie of friends in SMA. I think that's the fun part about a life that includes a ton of travel and is shrouded in an Everywhere Mindset: you can recreate yourself at any moment. I tend to be a very structured and driven person, so traveling and meeting new people allows me to loosen that grip—when you travel, you don't just experience those cultures; you experience *yourself* there as something or someone a little different. It's really freeing!

I created a busy life for myself in SMA. I'd work with the sculptor during the day and then meet up with my crew in the late afternoon: a retired cop from Chicago, a boyfriend from Mexico City, and a gaggle of art students who were always up for adventures to Taboada, the local hot springs. But I'm always drawn first and foremost to the entrepreneurs anywhere I go, so deep down, my favorite friends were all the side hustlers and solopreneurs who were making it happen there in non-traditional ways.

This time in SMA ignited my love of Mexico. The people, the culture, the history—it's just so different from the US, even though it's one of our closest neighbors. I found myself developing a real connection to the place, and I wanted to ensure that I could spend more time there in the future, so when the opportunity to buy property in Mexico presented itself, I was all in.

The coastline in the state of Oaxaca is stunning and much less touristy than places like Cancun or Acapulco or Cabo. The ocean is rough with riptides, and the services are rather basic, so it attracts a certain type of traveler—more surfers and fewer fancy resort-goers. That made for a great local community and vibe. At the time, there were several plots of land for sale adjacent to the beach, the only requirement being that purchasers needed to be Mexican. So, a group of international friends (including a couple born in Mexico) and I formed a limited liability company (LLC) and purchased several plots in a rural, waterfront beach cove called La Boquilla.

Our La Boquilla beach community was a rather ambitious project, especially since we were a large group of individual friends making decisions as a collective. Every year, we would make the trek from our respective homes around the world to La Boquilla for a week of plotting and planning the construction of our dream beach home. This became a fun yearly tradition (babies were born and marriages were formed and unformed during this time, among many other notable life events) but sadly, we never had the money or energy to build.

But what could have been a disappointment (letting that property sit unbuilt) turned into a blessing in disguise for me personally. Since there are no direct flights to our property in La Boquilla from the US, I'd fly through Mexico City every year with a stopover.

꿔꿔

Around 2016, I started to hear murmurs about the startup scene in CDMX (as Mexico City is often referred to); Techstars, the startup accelerator firm at which I'd become managing director two years prior, had an office there, so I got good intel about what was happening in the area. En route to La Boquilla, I started planning week-long stops in CDMX, working from the Techstars office and befriending my Latin American teammates who worked in that office. They were always super welcoming, and since it was challenging for them to get senior people from the company (who all lived in the US) to visit, they would set up lots of meetings and tote me around to various events.

I loved this because, as both a traveler and investor, my wheelhouse is being on the ground with locals, and I hoped my immersion would help build better bridges (partnerships, capital, customers) to the US. I'd encourage many of the local founders I met to apply to the various Techstars programs in the US, and then I'd quietly help them ace their applications and interviews. (Shush, I didn't just tell you that.) Being tightly connected to the local ecosystem and seeing it develop in real time also helped inform the thesis for my fund, Everywhere Ventures, where we partner closely with founders and investors who are local rather than thinking that we, as outsiders, know best.

Over the next few years of visiting Mexico City, I witnessed a gradual and then explosive rise in the tech ecosystem as the country produced some amazing companies, like Kavak (a marketplace for buying and selling used cars, whose founder I profile later in this chapter), Clip (payment solutions for small and medium-sized businesses), and Grin (electric scooters for urban mobility), among dozens of others.

The rise of the startup community there made sense in the context of many other developing tech ecosystems. Mexico had the perfect mix of a youthful and skilled workforce, plenty of tech talent flooding out of top engineering schools, co-working spaces galore, and several good incubators and accelerators. We all know that as the quality of startups increases, the presence of venture firms also increases, and in this case, it was venture capitalists from across Latin America and the US all rushing in. Mexico City's diverse and dynamic cultural environment (plus the food, drinks, and general hospitality) adds vibrancy to its tech ecosystem, attracting talent from all over.

Over the years, I became more and more enamored with all of it: the art and culture with diverse and interesting people to match. One of the highlights of my visits was sampling all the new local restaurants. CDMX has developed one of the best food scenes in the world, and the Techstars team took pride in how many good places were located just a few blocks from the office in the buzzy Roma Norte area. They took me to decadent lunches, where I would inevitably overeat and then need to walk back to the office just to stay awake for the rest of the day, and we'd have dinners in Polanco in places like Siembra, originally a tortilla shop and *taquería* that has blossomed into a corn haven, showcasing nixtamal tanks and *comales* in its open kitchen environment.

Then there was the very memorable Startup Weekend event taking place in the town of Tequila (if that tells you anything). This had not been pre-planned; when the organizers of the event heard that I was in Guadalajara (a ninety-minute drive from Tequila) for a work trip, they asked me to attend as a mentor and judge. I absolutely love doing things like this, so I didn't hesitate to say yes.

When I arrived at the event two days later, I discovered the programming was entirely in Spanish; I probably should've known that, but it hadn't occurred to me. Typically,

I can muddle through a dinner party, but beyond that, not so much. I did the best I could using my best "Spanglish" and speaking entirely in the present tense, for hours at a time, in front of a very eager audience of kids working on their start-ups. Thank goodness for Google Translate.

During a break in the event, the organizers took all the judges on a private tour of Jose Cuervo's original home to sample many, *many* types of tequila over the course of two hours. I'm not much of a drinker, but who am I to turn down such an experience?

When we got back to the event space, though, I learned that we still had two more hours of mentoring participants and then judging the final presentations, which was…rough.

Everyone said that my Spanish greatly improved, and that I sounded like a local for the rest of the day, which was a huge win—nothing like a little (or a lot of) tequila to help with fluency. And that, my friends, is another part of the Everywhere Mindset: going with the flow, even if the flow is about a gallon of a local delicacy called tequila!

KINETIC is the pillar of the Everywhere Mindset which captures the deep desire to explore the unknown. Full of energy, enthusiasm, and charisma, kinetic types tend to be fast to learn and faster to act, though they prefer to have the necessary data to act as decisively as possible. The word is derived from the Greek "kinetiko," meaning "motion," which is fitting, because when you interact with a kinetic person, you often feel their literal and figurative energy. Applied to entrepreneurship, the kinetic founder is the fast founder—a high-cadence thinker who moves quickly and acts on data as soon as relevant patterns emerge. They are ready to explore new ideas and methodologies and are not stuck in preconceived notions. Why this matters: a person

must seek out and find opportunities, as they may not be right in front of them.

KINETIC IN ACTION:

» *Adventure to places beyond your usual comfort zone.* I got on a plane to live and study in Mexico without knowing anyone or even having a place to stay. This was my first real solo adventure, and it pushed the boundaries of my comfort level as a young person fresh out of university. But going one level deeper, I was also taking a risk by exploring and encouraging my creative side, which I hadn't focused on during my rigorous university years.

» *Manufacture serendipity.* I did this by sitting in the cafe in the center of town in San Miguel Allende, putting myself in the flow and talking to people, which yielded friends, a place to live, and a "buzzy-ness" around me. I could have gone to Mexico and chilled, but I created a thriving life in a few short months. It's also worth noting that I'm an introvert, so being overly friendly and talking to random people does not come naturally to me.

» *Jump on opportunities once you see the signs (data) that things are working.* This was me buying property in a remote area which later became a hotspot and also recognizing that the Mexico City startup scene was going to take off and making it a priority to visit on my way to the property whenever I could.

LOREANNE GARCIA, CO-FOUNDER OF KAVAK

On one of my yearly trips to Mexico City, a colleague offered to pick me up at the airport, showing up in a cute Mini Cooper with racing stripes. It delighted me, as I had a very similar car back home. He told me that he'd bought it when he moved to Mexico through a used car marketplace that had recently launched in the country. On my next trip, I noticed that he had a different, bigger car; he had traded in the Mini, needing more room because he'd recently had a child. When I asked, he told me about Kavak, a platform launched by a brother-sister duo to make it easy and reliable to buy and sell used cars online in different cities and markets—something very new and novel to Mexico.

Years later, I was so excited to sit down with Kavak co-founder Loreanne Garcia, backing up to hear about her road to startup life.

Loreanne was born and raised in Venezuela, but her father was a high-level officer in the Venezuelan Navy, which meant their family moved frequently, often to different foreign locations, including stints in the United States.

Constantly immersed in different experiences and cultures and languages made for a peak Everywhere Mindset from early childhood, which endured into Loreanne's college years. There, she joined and led various groups including, importantly, the Young Entrepreneurs Business Association, of which she eventually became president (a harbinger of things to come).

At the same time, because of a major change in Venezuela's political situation, Loreanne's family's circumstances also shifted, and they all needed to (as she described it to me) "grow up very fast." She started working as an intern, her brother got a scholarship and joined the workforce, and her mom started a business.

Scattered and as tumultuous as it may have been for her, Loreanne finished university and took a job with Procter and Gamble, where she tapped into her own way to take action in response to what was happening in her homeland: "The best thing I can do is leave, get more prepared, and come back better." She decided to go elsewhere—not only for her safety but also to gather resources so she could either return to Venezuela or effect change there.

Her peripatetic life sped up further when Loreanne navigated to a role as a McKinsey consultant. She was based in Venezuela but traveled worldwide because, she explained, "there were no opportunities or projects in Venezuela" at the time. Part of her job was sitting down with CEOs, which, she said, "changed the way my mind worked." From there, she got into Stanford Business School, which *really* changed the way her mind worked.

Along the way, Loreanne started listening more closely to entrepreneurship stories, connecting with business owners, and getting more involved with the startup arm at McKinsey— which meant, in particular, mentorship with social entrepreneurs. This really clicked for her.

When she arrived at Stanford, Loreanne knew that it was the place she was *really* going to learn. "I saw the connections—it was amazing," she told me. "The energy there was everything."

Loreanne had to go back to McKinsey to repay her student loan, but before doing so, she couldn't resist her first startup attempt—a platform to help volunteers and donors give time and money to causes, reflecting her newly-formed drive around companies espousing impact.

That attempt failed, but all was not lost. Loreanne met her husband at Stanford, and in short order, moved with him to San Francisco to resume working at McKinsey (the Venezuela office had since shuttered), and then they finally moved on to Mexico, where they settled to raise a family.

Change is in Loreanne's DNA, or at least in her upbringing, so as a true subscriber to the Everywhere Mindset, she thrives in seemingly any environment. But the move to Mexico was the real catalyst for her startup spirit to ignite in earnest. She was drawn to something akin to entrepreneurship but was still mired in the corporate path for the time being, so she began working in microfinance (not a startup, per se, but a smaller company).

"After that, this entrepreneurship thing was burned in my mind forever," Loreanne explained. "Also, my brother and I always wanted to do something together. We're very different, but we complement each other very well."

Carlos was a visionary guy, Loreanne told me, coming up with new product ideas constantly while simultaneously advancing his more traditional career (also as a McKinsey consultant). When he transferred to Mexico, he had the idea for Kavak because he couldn't find an easy way to sell his barely-used car.

The problem to solve in hand, Carlos and Loreanne sat on it for a full two years, continuing on their separate professional paths as ideas percolated.

Carlos eventually decided to move forward with Kavak, and though she wasn't sure she wanted to work on it full-time, Loreanne started attending meetings, got super excited about it, and finally joined.

Even though she had been leaning in the direction of startups, it was still a pretty big leap to go from a steady paycheck and the prestige and structure of a bigger corporate role. I asked Loreanne what that final spur was for her.

As it turned out, having her first baby put her priorities in place. "I come from this hardcore corporate culture where you're supposed to work like crazy," she said. "And then when

I had a baby, I thought, *This is not going to work. I need to try to build a different world where I can still make an impact but do it in a different way.*"

Plus, Loreanne had adopted that "go big or go home" mentality—if she was going to take the risk of founding a company, she wanted to take a big risk for a big reward. I see this in a lot of founders, and I can relate. One way or another, we all get comfortable with taking the big swing at some point.

Being an only child, I was also intrigued about how the dynamic between siblings (for more, see Chapters 4 and 7) worked for Loreanne and Carlos as Kavak picked up steam.

"It was so much fun," she exclaimed, but added, "Of course, it's also very stressful because you are invested with this family member in a few different ways—personal and professional. But we learned to manage it and communicate our needs early on."

They found and cultivated resources outside their unit too. Loreanne told me their investors and organizations like Endeavor (a global community of and for high-impact entre-preneurs) were really helpful in the early years, helping them forge connections to create a web of support.

More important, perhaps, was that they structurally set the company—and themselves—up properly, with a clear deline-ation around strengths, roles, and responsibilities. Loreanne and Carlos, along with their third co-founder, Roger, started and stayed in their own lanes in the business: Carlos as CEO, Roger in operations and commercial, and Loreanne work-ing on everything HR-related, as well as legal, finance, and back office.

"That was one of the most important things for us to be successful," Loreanne told me. "From day one we said, 'How are we going to split this up?' And it was very clear."

It was also, said Loreanne, built entirely on trust—perhaps of a deeper variety that can be found among some siblings more readily.

All of this resonated with who I was learning Loreanne was, fundamentally, as a person. The first time we were scheduled to talk for this interview, she asked to reschedule because someone on her team had a family situation come up and she wanted to be present for them.

It makes sense, then, that at Kavak she would take on everything relating to their employees. "People on the team make the culture. They're the ones moving everything in the business forward," she noted.

That brand of empathy—which threads throughout her career—also certainly contributes to her ability to be an incredible leader.

"I've heard the word leadership since I was a year old," Loreanne told me. "My dad was in the Navy—and while you probably imagine him as very strict, very disciplined, that wasn't the case. No, he was a very different leader. He always cared about people, cared about people being happy, being productive. So, I think leadership was just something that was always there, not something I figured out later." She added, "I'm a very collaborative leader. I like to listen. I like to make sure that people are in the roles that make their eyes shine. I'm very human-oriented."

She also shared that she learned how to communicate when she was very young, which helped her as a leader; her mom had taken a class in public speaking at one point, and she was always teaching those principles to Loreanne and Carlos.

It was so interesting to hear from Loreanne because so many of the entrepreneurs I work with are not only charismatic, they're also fantastic speakers. People want to be around that energy, and it only adds to the founder's success.

For Loreanne and Kavak, that happened, in part, by focusing on what mattered, which, she said, is the people—especially the customers. "Before you launch, you have to listen to various people," explained Loreanne. "Then you have to *not* listen to anyone except your customer for a while."

That 360-degree people-focus really seemed to draw a direct line to Kavak's success—the company achieved unicorn status (a valuation of over one billion dollars) in 2020, and it is currently the largest such company in all of Latin America. I can't emphasize enough how impressive this is—Kavak is a huge deal in Mexico (and increasingly, in other geographies) and has a higher valuation than most US unicorns.

But there's also an incredible amount of intensity (and pressure) attached to that designation, and I wanted to understand how Loreanne keeps things in perspective, so I asked her how she stayed grounded through everything. "I think your mind is one of the most powerful things, and I had to learn how to control mine," she said, then added with a laugh, "Also, admitting that every day is going to be crazy. Before, I used to think, *It's just the next three months; they're going to be crazy*, and then it's the next three months. But it doesn't stop. I learned how to live with that in a healthy way."

"Before being an entrepreneur," she said, "I spent a lot of time thinking about what I could and couldn't do, trying to figure out my limits. But when you're actually doing it, you start growing and don't even realize it. Then you stop and realize, *Oh wow, that was me a year ago, and this is me now.*"

Loreanne continued, "How did this happen? Because all the time and energy I used to spend or waste thinking about those things, I'm now using to build and move forward. And that's something that I didn't know I could do before."

Plenty of founders focus on personal growth and development by way of mindfulness out of interest or necessity, and Loreanne obviously did that too. But her story and trajectory also revealed a profound truth about the unique illumination entrepreneurship offers *to* a person's growth path and *as* a growth path itself.

KEY INSIGHTS:
LOREANNE AS A KINETIC FOUNDER

» *Explore—and be open to augment your adaptability.* Due to her father's career, Loreanne moved almost yearly to a new place with her family. This might have been traumatic for a different type of person, but her kinetic nature embraced those new environments, creating all sorts of positive and exciting opportunities.

» *Seek contagious kinetic energy.* Loreanne decided to go to Stanford, a long way from her home and family back in Venezuela, where the entrepreneurial energy inspired her and spurred forward momentum toward her first company, as did meeting other fast-thinking students. Being surrounded by people who share your enthusiasm can be a catalyst for innovation and non-consensus thinking.

» *Embrace leadership through communication skills.* Loreanne showed that being kinetic was more than just physical or energetic but also intellectual, anchored in her people-forward approach to business. She started developing those skills from a young age as the president of the Young Entrepreneurs Business Association and then later as the head of human resources at Kavak. But for the rest of us, it's never too late to start!

CHAPTER 2

INDIA

I f you've read the book *Eat, Pray, Love*, you already know the story of a heartbroken woman from New York City who shows up at an ashram near Mumbai, India, to "find herself." In my case, it was an Ashtanga yoga school in Mysore in South India. But it's a similar idea.

As a type-A New Yorker, traditional meditation is tough for me. The idea of sitting quietly and concentrating on one thing runs contrary to the forty-two tabs I have open at any given moment in my computer's browser and the go-go-go lifestyle that I live.

But in the early-2000s, when I walked into my very first Ashtanga yoga class in the East Village and the instructor talked about "exhausting the body to quiet the mind," it all clicked. For years after, I'd rise early to go through the Ashtanga poses, and I carried my yoga mat with me everywhere—taking any opportunity that presented itself to break into a sun salutation. In fact, I once found myself moving through the *asanas* at JFK when my flight was delayed six hours and I had another ten-hour flight ahead of me (giving literal meaning to the Everywhere Mindset—or perhaps in this case, Everywhere Yoga!). People stared a bit, but because it was New York City, I was not the weirdest stranded passenger.

Ashtanga yoga—which is a more energetic form of practice, matching movement to breath—tends to attract a certain type of personality, including extreme athletes, marathoners, and other intense people like hedge fund managers. So, that yoga community deviates from the stereotypical "kumbaya" hippie-types and includes many more hard-driving individuals who seem to benefit from that type of time on the yoga mat.

I had known several yoga students who had made the trek to Mysore to study with a well-known yoga teacher credited with bringing Ashtanga yoga to the West. I'd also heard he was getting up there in age and I should go soon to experience the yoga *shala* (which means "home" in Sanskrit) there.

The next thing you know, I'd dropped off everything I owned at the local thrift store and boarded a flight to India, carrying nothing more than a tiny knapsack.

Upon arrival at the yoga shala in Mysore, each yoga student is assigned a time slot to practice, and mine was at 5:00 a.m. each morning. So, at 4:30 a.m., I'd grab my roommate, Colin (a 6'4" artist-turned-psychotherapist from Boston), jump onto the handlebars of his bike (we only had one to share, and his legs were longer), and navigate around cows and goats on the unpaved back roads to the studio. Like many first timers to India, nothing prepared me for the total sensory overload when I first arrived—the cows, the colors, and the curry-scented air all came at me fast and furiously.

The other option was to find a rickshaw driver, but at that hour, the conversation and constant negotiating over price was just too annoying. It was always 200 rupees to the shala, and each morning they'd quote me 400 rupees until I physically walked away from the vehicle, at which point, they'd agree to the usual 200-rupee price. Rinse, repeat—and most days it was even the same driver.

By 7:00 a.m., we were finished with our practice—exhausted and famished—so we'd head back into town to what was locally known as The Sisters house (run by, as the name suggests, three sisters), which became one of our favorite places in India.

Over the years, many of the local women in Mysore got wind of the presence of international yoga students and opened their homes to us for meals. For breakfast, they made homemade granola (not something they ate themselves) and served it with yogurt and fresh fruit, since that's what the yoga students ate. As we sat on pillows on the floor discussing our plans for the day, the kids in the neighborhood would peer in curiously at our bowls full of foreign food and giggle as we tried to engage them in conversation. The Sisters had somehow procured an industrial-grade juicer, making it all the rage with the yoga students who queued up all morning as they pumped out fresh mango and green juice from their kitchen window by the gallons.

After that, the morning activity was swimming and hiding from the heat at the pool of the local Star of India hotel, where the more affluent families in town also took their children for swimming lessons. The anxious mothers (many of whom did not swim) would stand at the side of the pool while the children shrieked with fear and delight about being thrown into the deep end. So, the background noise of our pool-lounging morning would be the instructor bellowing at the kids to "Stroke! Stroke! Stroke!" for hours on end. But sometimes, the kids would get the last laugh when the mean instructor would end up soaking wet, having been inadvertently splashed by a kid with a really aggressive stroke!

Other daytime activities included studying Sanskrit, taking cooking classes, and designing clothing with the local tailors. They have incredible tailors and fabrics, and it's *the* local activity, plus it's super affordable. In fact, as soon as I arrived in India, I noticed a very distinct type of woven, waxy bag that everyone carried all their yoga props in (which I later started spotting in NYC and Los Angeles). We called them Mysore bags, and when I was there, we made them by the dozens. Given this new custom of tailoring I was immersed in, I planned to transform my black-and-gray minimalist uniform into a shimmering cascade of pink and orange robes. Remember, part of the Everywhere Mindset is about embracing new cultures, and that includes their clothing!

The dark side of all that yoga is that many students end up injured or with aches and pains at some point during their time in Mysore. I was no different. The yoga is physically intense, and they push you really hard at the *shala*, so as soon as my hip started to ache, I knew it was time to move on.

It was hard to leave the cast of characters and the daily routine I'd pieced together over my three months living in Mysore, so on my final night, we all gathered for a special *thali* dinner at the magical Green Hotel.

Though I was ready to leave Mysore and the yoga school, I wasn't ready to re-enter my life in New York, so I spent the next two months traveling the country from south to north, exploring and meeting up with friends, and friends of friends, along the way. But the side trip I most looked forward to was spending a few weeks in Dharmsala in the Himalayas for Losar—the Tibetan New Year—when people decorate their houses, make traditional food, and enjoy the local music. It's a really special and festive time.

As an undergraduate student at Columbia University, I became interested in Buddhism after taking a class on Indo-Tibetan Buddhist Studies with Professor Robert Thurman. I loved the class (as many students did) and was introduced to several principles and teachings that resonated with me. One of my favorites was the idea of radical individualism, which was explained to me as not having to be a doctor just because your father was one and not having to conform to your tribe more generally.

That spoke to me in a way nothing else ever had and became the blueprint for my "non-traditional" and travel-oriented life. Professor Thurman had also spent time with the Dalai Lama and encouraged his students to visit Dharamshala during the New Year celebrations to receive his public teachings. I couldn't wait to see everything that had resonated so deeply with me.

I arrived in McLeod Ganj, a suburb of Dharamshala where the Dalai Lama lives, after an overnight train from Delhi with a family of five. The parents were on the bottom bunk, three kids were in the middle bunk, and I was up on top in the third berth. There was fighting, video games, and the mother serving up freshly made *chapati* from an actual hot plate literally all night long. Needless to say, that wasn't my best night's sleep.

In typical Jenny style, when I impulsively jumped on that train from New Delhi to the Himalayas, I hadn't realized that showing up without a hotel reservation during the high season of Losar was not advisable. Yet, as also tends to happen with me when I travel, luck was on my side; while every hotel was fully booked out for months, one of the hotel proprietors took pity on me and offered me a unique situation—a freestanding tent on the roof of the hotel that was usually inhabited by hotel staff.

I was thrilled just to have a place to rest (and the tent was surprisingly roomy with a dresser and a rug), and as it turned out, it was a great spot, perfectly situated on the cliff looking down into the Kangra valley. Also, since just about everyone could see my tent from the center of town, people started referring to me as "tent-girl," and very quickly, my reputation in that remote location preceded me.

Every morning, I'd practice yoga on the roof of the hotel, which I point out here for two reasons. One, because even though I was constantly setting out on travel adventures, I always toted along with me a rigid plan and created structure and routine wherever I went. Two, I knew I had an audience up there on the roof. Slowly, people started to come join me, with over twenty people at the height. But these were not just ordinary people who came to do yoga—they were mostly monks! You see, during Losar, thousands of Tibetan monks come from around the world to McLeod Ganj to hear the Dalai Lama, and the town is awash in a sea of red and yellow robes. Many of these monks are in exile, living in India and Nepal, and, not surprisingly, they were naturals at Ashtanga yoga. Each day after morning yoga, we'd roll into English lessons (they were quick to learn), and after a hearty lunch of traditional Tibetan *momo* dumplings, we'd all head over to hear the teachings broadcast on the lawn outside of the Dalai Lama's residence.

One morning, while sitting on the roof and gazing down into the valley, I thought about Professor Thurman and his lecture on radical individualism in college. Although I had fought it initially by going to law school and working in finance, it was abundantly clear that my path was going in a different direction—one that would deviate significantly from my peers and my tribe.

I would make it back home to NYC a month later, but the truth is that I was never really going back to my old life.

༉༅

In 2015, I was on a Google Hangout with a founder in Bangalore who was pitching me his new startup. I was interested in the concept (3D scanning solutions for dentists) but assumed the infrastructure in India was still as fragile as I remembered it and that the complexity of his business would be challenged because of it. But the founder persisted despite my skepticism, and at some point, the doorbell rang. He excused himself for one moment, reaching for his mobile phone and letting in the Flipkart delivery guy without ever getting up off his chair. He apologized and explained that he had ordered some groceries right before our call and didn't expect them to arrive so quickly. As he continued with his pitch, I thought to myself, *Holy wow, that was even faster delivery than Amazon in New York!*

Clearly, something very interesting was happening in India on the startup scene, and I needed to check it out for myself.

Although Techstars didn't have an accelerator program or office in India yet, it did have one or two employees in the region who ran the community events like Startup Weekend. I messaged them about coming to visit, and they were excited to introduce me to the local tech community.

Running the accelerator program really was the perfect job for me because as long as I delivered top results, I had autonomy over most everything, including my budget. While some managing directors allocated their budgets for things like founder retreats, year-round offices, or more staff members, I spent a good chunk of my budget traveling the world finding and recruiting founders—bringing the best startups into my program was not only my job but it was also my passion, and I was really good at it.

When I arrived in Bangalore, I was shocked by the myriad of noticeable changes since my last trip and realized my perception of Indian infrastructure was completely outdated.

In fact, Bangalore had leapfrogged many countries in terms of the basics like highways, high-rise buildings, high-speed Wi-Fi, and an international airport (although it's worth noting that today, it's struggling with congestion and water issues). These are the types of small yet huge details that make doing business in a far-flung place easier and thus, more accessible.

Bangalore had arguably become the tech center of the country and one of the fastest-developing and most vibrant (especially when it comes to business) cities, and this trip, I was spending time there as a founder with an exit under my belt and a career as a venture capitalist—so no flowing red robes or yoga classes for me. The trip was a revelation, and I felt it in my bones that we needed to launch an accelerator program there. So, as soon as I touched down at JFK, I called up David Cohen, the CEO and co-founder of Techstars, and made my argument for Techstars moving quickly into the region. After my ten-minute impassioned monologue, there was a beat, and then David calmly explained to me that plans were already in the works for an office, a program, and a corporate innovation center. He was, as usual, many steps ahead of me (and everyone).

Many years later, when my co-founder, Scott, and I started Everywhere Ventures, we discovered we both had lived in India at similar times, me studying yoga and him working at the Google office there. Originating from those different perspectives, we came together with our desire to tap into the startup scene and invest there.

But investing in India is complex with strict international investment rules, so we had to get creative (and of course, Systematic) in entering the country and recruiting our investment committee and limited partner base. For us, that usually means working with other venture capitalists and contacts on the ground in each place to add into our investment thesis. Luckily, we both had deep connections to the continent and were able to create a plan and rally a strong team to help us with our global expansion.

The SYSTEMATIC component of the Everywhere Mindset means being methodical and structured, complete with a roadmap and plan as part of a larger set of principles. Systematics thrive on precision and predictability. Rather than being especially animated and relying on charisma,

they look for data and patterns to point to the answers and iterate from there. Many Systematics in the startup world have backgrounds as engineers, who often think in systems, approaching problems as part of a broader dynamic system (which is how coding works). Typically, cooler heads prevail—Systematics are not often overly emotional or thrown off course when things don't go well, (or do), so they are masters at getting things done.

SYSTEMATIC IN ACTION:

» ***Rinse and repeat.*** Practice, of course, leads to improvement and better outcomes, and repetition frees up mental space to do other things. I saw this very clearly with my Ashtanga practice, which is a daily routine consisting of a set grouping of poses that never changes, meant to exhaust my body and quiet my mind.

» ***Have a plan within the plan.*** The importance of careful planning and preparation before taking action can't be denied. Some of my travel might seem impulsive, but it was far from unstructured or unplanned, as evidenced, for example, by the amount of preparation I undertook before arriving in India to meet startups for my program.

» ***Cut your losses.*** Systematics love data as a signpost for moving forward, but it also helps them see reality, understand when things aren't working, and move on when warranted, much like when I started to experience pain from doing too much yoga and knew it was time to stop.

ABHISHEK GOYAL AND NEHA SINGH, CO-FOUNDERS OF TRACXN

Abhishek Goyal, founder of Tracxn, a research platform for investors, embarked on his entrepreneurial journey following a roadmap deeply rooted in his ancestry. Growing up in Jodhpur amidst the rich cultural tapestry (and beauty!) of India, he inherited a legacy from his Marwadi lineage—a community renowned for its entrepreneurial acumen in building businesses across the country, particularly in commerce.

And though a lot of Marwadis eschewed education for their kids, believing it would derail them from family businesses, Abhishek's entrepreneurial DNA was augmented by his education at good schools, which his parents fully encouraged. Education, he told me, was "the easiest way to earn a very graceful life," and for him, it was a means to an end. That end was Tracxn, but along the way there was *so* much more.

Abhishek studied computer science, not out of interest, but because it was the norm for people like him who ranked so high academically. Becoming a founder had already taken hold, though, as the way of life for him, an integral piece to his whole narrative.

"There's a popular joke among the Marwadi community," Abhishek said, "that when they go to a restaurant, instead of enjoying the food, they try to figure out just how profitable the restaurant is. Business permeated every aspect of my young life—even food!"

Upon graduating in 2002, Abhishek held a variety of engineering roles at big companies like Yahoo, Amazon, and 3i, but he was also working on a few startup ideas on the side. By the time he joined the Indian arm of the prominent venture capital firm Accel, he had six or seven attempts at company creation under his belt.

Around that time, Abhishek told me, his ambition was to start something that could "maybe pay the salaries of ten people and become a stable shop."

But joining Accel taught him what large businesses mean to the world, what they can do, and more importantly, how to build them. His big win was sourcing Flipkart, an e-commerce company that's among the biggest Indian tech success stories. At the time, it wasn't a popular deal at Accel, and I could sense that Abhishek needed to pound the table in order to make the investment. But by age twenty-eight, he'd written the first check into Flipkart, buying twenty-five percent of the company for less than a million dollars.

"That added multiple decimals to multiple zeros to what my ambition looked like before that," Abhishek told me with a smile.

Then in 2010, it was time: Abhishek started his own e-commerce company called Urban Touch (selling jewelry, beauty products, handbags, etc.) which was backed by the venture capital funds, Tiger and Accel, a big win for a young entrepreneur.

Until it wasn't.

The company found itself in a difficult spot—a "funding winter" as Abhishek described it—and ended up selling to another e-commerce startup, Fashion and You, and only returned a portion of capital to shareholders. In the world of venture capital, only the billion dollar exits move the needle for large funds like Accel or Tiger, and everything else is considered a failure.

Abhishek had been at the top of his game—as a student, as a VC, then founding a venture-backed company at a young age. But things didn't turn out how he'd expected, and since I have had similar experiences (of the right-idea-wrong-time variety), I asked him how he processed that disappointment.

"At that time, I didn't think too much about it, because by then, I had seen so many startups fail, I felt like it was part of the equation," he explained. "But looking back much later, I thought I could have done a lot of things differently."

Although his first startup didn't pan out, one thing did, which was his relationship with Neha Singh, who happened to be on a parallel path at Sequoia Capital India, the offshoot of the famed Silicon Valley-based venture capital fund.

After meeting, they bonded over a common point of interest—they had both individually developed their own system to help them do their jobs more easily and efficiently. In the most illustrative example of the "empath" founder(s), they merged their personal lives and their business interests, coming up with the idea for Tracxn so they could do their jobs better by becoming even more systematic.

Along with Abhishek, I was excited to also be able to speak with Neha for *Venture Everywhere*, and in that conversation, she told me, "It's not that I wanted to be an entrepreneur or that I was looking for an idea. It was just that this idea filled a huge gap in the market and was compelling enough to pursue."

彡彡

In 2015, while working at Techstars in NYC, I started receiving cold emails from a guy named Anoop. He claimed to be able to help me with my outbound startup deal sourcing. The emails were personalized, and Anoop seemed to know concisely the pain points for venture capital fund managers like me. I didn't respond (at least at first), but I always read his emails—and clearly, he could see that I was opening them, so he continued to correspond.

One day, I responded, and that simple act of clicking "Reply" set off a firehose of marketing emails coming at me fast and furious. At some point, I stopped hearing from Anoop, but I did hear from Shubham, Mohit, and Somaiah. I appreciated their persistence, good nature (never too pushy), and perfect grammar, and although I never purchased their product, I became curious about the company and its origins. I learned that the founders were a husband-and-wife team (Abhishek and Neha, obviously). They'd started the company in India in 2013 but knew that the US and EMEA were going to be big markets for them (70 percent of their business comes from outside of India), so they set up the company with a global footprint (and an Everywhere Mindset) from day one. This is not an easy path for any startup with limited resources and bandwidth, but it's definitely an ambitious one that many investors appreciate.

Tracxn is a research firm that provides information and startup data for venture capitalists and corporate development offices. They use big data and artificial intelligence to track companies across 250-plus technology sectors in 30-plus countries. Customers include prominent VCs and corporates such as Matrix Partners, Social Capital, and Fujitsu. Today, Tracxn is among the world's top five private market data providers and is similar to Pitchbook, Crunchbase, and CB Insights. It wasn't a surprise to me that Tracxn is backed by some of the best venture capitalists and angel investors in the world like Accel, Sequoia Capital, and even the founders of Flipkart, who were excited to support Abhishek. Tracxn aims to revolutionize startup research with its global outlook and innovative approach.

As I mentioned earlier, the company started from Abhishek and Neha's own personal needs as former investment associates in venture funds, where research was a fundamental part of sourcing and closing deals, but so much of it was analog and repetitive. That became the starting point.

Neha got a scholarship to the MBA program at Stanford, figuring if they did end up launching the company, it would be the perfect hub to make things easier for them via the resources and networks found there. Then, for over two years while she was studying in Palo Alto, they debated the merits of the Tracxn idea and whether it was big enough to succeed. Indeed, it was. They eventually started the company together, and though it might have been a "side hustle" for them at the time, its global ambition was evident from the beginning.

The first product they launched was for the US market, not for the Indian market. And since Abhishek and Neha were both VCs, concepts like total addressable market (TAM) and moat (a competitive advantage) were important to them in everything they did.

"We always said that whatever we do, it has to be global in nature. Because if you start with India, then even if you capture the Indian market, everybody will keep questioning the total market size," he told me. "And later, expanding can take its own time and (have its own) challenges. We were always sure that we had to have global customers. So very early on we had customers in twenty or thirty countries. Today, we have customers in fifty-plus countries."

So, for Tracxn, total addressable market was the global ambition, and moat (a point of differentiation or long-term competitive advantage from what existed in the market) pushed them to only launch features where they thought defensibility was very high to keep their competitive advantage.

In a variety of ways, Abhishek is a self-proclaimed "calculator" when it comes to business, and that helped him balance all the things a founder needs to balance on this crazy journey, like self-confidence and humility, as well as decisiveness with vulnerability.

"For me it came very naturally as a Marwadi," he said. "We're from business families; we are always listening; we are always calculating things. And when I'm right, I know I'm right, because I have done a lot of calculations. I have figured out that this is the thing to do."

Neha and Abhishek also calculated a few bold calls during their building process. For example, they ended up shutting down their US office—which was their largest market at the time—because the numbers didn't add up to viability. Abhishek said, "When I see numbers, I follow the data not the emotion."

If his confidence came from the numbers, I wondered where his resilience came from. As it turned out, it came from continuous setbacks.

"The biggest idea can be misunderstood by the smartest people for a few years—it's okay to hear no," he explained, reminding me that his original claim to fame, the Flipkart deal, had been dismissed before becoming a mind-blowing success.

"So now I don't find it unsettling that nobody agrees with me," he said, laughing. "I love it."

Neha clearly shared his confidence and conviction. When we spoke, she told me, "We *were* the customers; I would love using this. From all angles, it just looked like a problem that we would love spending our life on. Second thing is that this is a customer segment we love working with—VCs and corporates."

One of the most interesting parts of the Tracxn story is their decision to take the company public at an early stage (at least by US standards) not long after raising their Series B round of funding. While this would not be possible on a US stock exchange, in India, the revenue and maturity standards are somewhat different, so it worked.

As I thought more about the idea of going public early, one thing I liked about it was how it gives retail investors a chance to get in at a lower price since the company is newer and smaller—something that is not readily available in the US, where private company investors need to be "accredited," and companies ready to list on the stock market need to be big. Of that decision, Neha explained, "We thought that this was a very interesting problem, and we could build a very deep and valuable business around it. While India had been a back-office hub for a lot of the financial data companies, it now had the potential to produce a product-focused data company." She continued, describing their reasoning behind a deviation from services businesses being built in India to a scalable product company: "Getting listed provides you the opportunity to continue to build and scale for the next decade."

Neha talked a bit more about what she sees as both a "propensity" for Indian companies to go public earlier (in the US, there are about 4,000 listed companies, and in India there are about 6,000 with more coming up the ladder) because it's more manageable over there—with less strict compliance and regulations like we see in the US. Plus, she noted, in India, there's a lot of investor interest, leading some companies to move to Indian markets.

But of course, that kind of bold move had a ton of challenges—any sort of scaling does, as I've seen hundreds of times in my work—and Abhishek explained his viewpoint that managing stakeholders was a key to their successful navigation of it all.

"Number one is hiring a good team who can work with you, being aligned 100 percent. Where they are treating the company like their home. They don't treat it like another job and just do nine-to-five. You want people who are committed *with* you," he told me.

And then he discussed managing external stakeholders, which his partner, (in business and life) Neha, did so well: "She did a lot of work with respect to managing shareholder alignment of interest." At the time of their IPO, Tracxn had 30,000 shares, and today they have over 80,000, making that skill exponentially more critical.

Neha told me that being mission-driven also helps—their true north, which was there from the beginning and multiplied by two—keeps them focused and going public meant taking a long-term view.

"You can be driven by short-term objectives," Neha said, "but doing and redoing things constantly, that's not worth it. Figure out what you want to solve in the long term and then work backwards."

🐉🐉

Toward the end of our conversation, Abhishek pinpointed an underlying truth, which is that "being a founder is a traumatic journey. It's not even a difficult journey, it's a *traumatic* journey."

Trauma stems from emotion, and he told me how as VCs, he and Neha saw things like a company growing like crazy, but then watched as the founders got stuck in a difficult spot and developed a very dark mindset.

For their part, Abhishek and Neha knew when they started Tracxn that this would be part of the journey—and being aware that those feelings would arise ironically helped them get through them that much faster. And for them, as both spouses and business partners, it came down to getting through everything together—for better or for worse.

Neha did tell me she initially thought entering into the startup journey solo, let alone together, was a risky financial decision. In fact, early on, they both tried to talk each other out of starting Tracxn—one then the other offered to take on the financial burden (of not having a stable job with a high income)—but they couldn't agree, so they pursued it together despite thinking it was a bad idea for them both to be working at a startup.

"We both really, *really* wanted to do it," Neha told me with a smile, "So we did it together."

Abhishek further illuminated the shared drive that neither of them could shake: "Your spouse matters a lot. In a lot of cases, stress compounds because your spouse cannot really understand the level of trauma you're going through and why you're going through it. In our case, both of us are doing the same thing, so we always understand."

He told me a story about a vacation they'd booked. At the last minute, an important meeting for Tracxn came up, and they had to cancel everything. Most other spouses—even if they themselves were businesspeople—would likely not be so understanding. But Neha and Abhishek turned the car around without a whiff of argument or struggle.

"Life becomes easier when the context is shared," he told me. They also, incidentally, share a love of—and deep commitment to—their fitness regiments. Neha especially is adamant that they're only able to do what they do so successfully (balance working together, a huge growth startup, and a growing family) by investing heavily in exercise and wellness.

And though Abhishek told me they're very disciplined in another area— "turning it off" at the end of the day so not everything is about work—I was curious to know if investors had been worried when they learned he and Neha were a married couple in addition to being co-founders.

In India specifically, "It was not common for spouses to start companies together—that was not seen as a good combination," he told me. "But I think over time, they saw we were professional, we didn't run it like a family business, we don't behave in the office like spouses, we behave like co-founders. I think how we behave really reduced a lot of that anxiety among people."

In defying traditional norms and demonstrating their professionalism, Abhishek and Neha seem to sidestep any landmines with their spouse-led ventures, earning the trust and respect of investors and employees alike. As Abhishek aptly summarized, the entrepreneurial path is not merely challenging—it's a transformative journey, marked by resilience, adaptability, and unwavering determination. And for Abhishek and Neha, I saw their shared and deep commitment to their vision, coupled with their alignment as quintessentially systematic thinkers and founders, continues to drive Tracxn's success, proving that true partnership knows no bounds. They're in it for the long game in all areas of their life.

KEY INSIGHTS:
ABHISHEK AND NEHA AS SYSTEMATIC FOUNDERS

» *Develop your own system.* Not all systems are created alike or equal, so you have to work within a structure that works for *you.* Neha and Abhishek's success was built upon the creation of their own proprietary system for improving their research abilities as VCs and led to the creation of their company Tracxn.

» *Look at all the angles.* Neha and Abhishek spent two years debating the merits of starting Tracxn (and then each tried to each talk the other out of doing so!), showcasing the importance of considering every component that would comprise the plan or system.

» *Create an open system.* An important part of Neha and Abhishek's ability to preside so well over their meteoric growth was the able management of all their myriad stakeholders. They did this by adhering to their vision and communicating it repeatedly until buy-in was achieved.

CHAPTER 3

UNITED KINGDOM

I had just shut down my second startup and was working on my next idea when I decided to take myself on a big trip, both for customer discovery purposes and for inspiration. For me, that means being in Everywhere-mode.

Though I'd planned about fifteen stops in different places, I only got as far as NYC to London.

I'd purchased a special around-the-world plane ticket, which at the time was only about $1,000 for as many stops as you want, provided you kept traveling in the same direction. My first touchdown was the UK, where I happened to end up at a dinner in London with a crew of executives from BBC Worldwide (the commercial arm of the British Broadcast Corporation, the quasi-government-supported media company), who were all brainstorming what the next big innovation would be; they had been early with products like iPlayer and BBC.com and now needed to stay ahead of the digital curve.

One of the things I love most about working as and with entrepreneurs is coming up with new ideas—of course, many (maybe most) don't stick, but it's so energizing to sit around a table tossing things out to see what resonates. At dinner, I was doing just that, giving the digital execs all sorts of ideas off the top of my head while eating upscale British pub food.

"You should come work with us!" one of the execs exclaimed.

I laughed, thinking they were joking. Spoiler alert: they were not.

At the time, I really had zero interest in taking a job or working at a big company, but they managed to get me to agree to a meeting, which became another meeting, which became me signing on to consult with them for three months (*Tops*, I told myself), helping form their strategy for the Digital Ventures group and assisting them in finding someone to run it.

Fast forward to me sitting with those same BBC execs in meeting after meeting with recruiters. Four meetings in, and with four more to go that day, they looked at me and said, "Jenny, *you* are the person for the role."

It's possible I wasn't necessarily the best person for the job, and they just couldn't stand meeting with any more recruiters that day, but either way, I ended up joining the team as the Head of Digital Ventures, making strategic venture capital investments for the company.

I hadn't anticipated this turn of events, but life apparently had other plans—and I was glad I took the job. I never even returned to NYC to pick anything up; I just started working with them after our initial dinner and ended up staying for more than three years! I really enjoyed the people who worked there; they all loved their work and the deeper mission behind the organization. This all showcases a critical part of the Everywhere Mindset: openness to—and excitement for—the complete unknown, even in other cultures and with things I had never even begun to imagine.

So, there I was, hunting for a flat in the middle of a snowstorm in January without a proper coat or winter boots. (I knew it tended toward rain, but I didn't quite realize I'd be facing that kind of winter weather in London!)

Luckily, a friend came to the rescue with a unique housing arrangement. She owned a flat in London but was currently living in Asia, and her subletter had fallen in love with a guy on a weekend trip to Croatia and never came back—not even to pick up her stuff. My friend was in a pinch to rent out the place but couldn't get back to London to clean it out right away. So, I moved right into someone else's life, and since I owned nothing, it was perfect! It was on Westbourne Grove in Notting Hill, and although I swore, I wouldn't be *that* typical American living in *that* area, it turns out that's exactly what I was.

And I loved every minute! The flat was in prime Notting Hill near Ledbury Road, an iconic street that had been chock full of uber-precious boutiques run by the wives of London investment bankers. When the Great Financial Crisis hit, all the shops closed, seemingly overnight. By the time I moved in, the fancy stores were starting to make a comeback, interspersed with the Oxfam charity shops that had filled in during the downturn, painting a much more interesting (in my opinion) and less vanilla snapshot of the streetscape.

﷽

While building startups, I had interacted with accelerator programs like Techstars (where I later worked as a Managing Director), Y Combinator, and Seedcamp, which provided necessary resources to inception-stage startups. I also knew of several strategic accelerator programs backed by large corporate brands in the US but wondered why there weren't any of these programs in the UK. In fact, I dug a little deeper, looking more widely across Europe, and still couldn't really find any.

Lightbulb moment: I came up with a concept called BBC Worldwide Labs (or just "Labs" for short), a strategic accelerator program where we would work with batches of European-based startups with the objective of helping them get pilots and partnerships within the various divisions of the BBC. In addition to investing in external companies, we were accelerating early ones, and I essentially became CEO of Labs. I really got that off the ground over the following few months by meeting with all the heads of the business units and getting them on board with this vision, and I had a blast doing it.

I spoke with all the consumer divisions like BBC News, BBC Food, BBC Earth, as well as the internal groups focused on advertising, technology, and compliance. If you ran a business unit, I was going to meet with you and figure out your needs and, more importantly, if you were willing to work with unproven, early-stage startups.

Then, I'd talk the business unit leader into becoming a "mentor" in the Labs program, and I'd add their headshot to the unofficial website that I created (this website was not blessed by the organization, I'm afraid, since I didn't want to wait to get it up and running, and anyway, I generally operated with an MO of proceed until apprehended, otherwise known as "ask for forgiveness, not permission"). Once I felt the exec in question was on board and emotionally invested in the program, I surmised I'd have an easier time getting them to *actually* help the startups. Aligning interests with a bit of positive manipulation is one of my superpowers!

I particularly admired the woman who ran the BBC Food division, so, for example, I ended up pairing her as a mentor with a startup that helped with menu planning and grocery shopping for busy families and professionals in the UK.

Labs became the first corporate accelerator in the UK, and to my knowledge, Europe. It went on for many years—well after I left—with hundreds of startups going through the program, which makes me very proud.

But I think the best thing about it was that it really activated the people who worked at the BBC: startups were becoming more prevalent, and people internally were hearing about the program, getting excited about it, and wanting to help out and be part of it, which was amazing. We developed a really engaged and engaging mentor pool from within the company—it catalyzed some serious internal momentum.

Culturally speaking, as a straight-talking, often brash American, I wasn't an obvious fit for a very proper British company, and I think I might have been fired for being so bold if it wasn't for the fact that my role was to be the face of everything entrepreneurial at the company. As an American, especially in 2010, everyone assumed I was ahead when it came to all things innovation, so I was given a lot of leeway.

In London, I didn't realize that when you went into a meeting, the first ten minutes were unofficially slated for a series of apologies (for being late, not prepared, or even for the weather), followed by more talk about the weather. I really had no idea what was going on and would kick off my meetings quickly with very little small talk, not realizing how abrupt and rude that felt to the Brits.

[Side note: Just between us, I also figured out a work-around for the clunky BBC IT login authentication system so I could use my personal Apple computer, which was frowned upon in such a large corporation. And now, a decade later, if you email jenny.fielding@bbc.com, I'll get your email. Give it a try—but please don't get me in trouble with the IT and compliance guys!]

But in all seriousness, I was thankful for the hall pass I got and for how everyone was so open and happy to meet with me and absorb some of that famous American entrepreneurial spirit.

To that end, it was a pretty exciting time in London as the startup scene grew, and since I'd gone through the early days of the same environment in New York, I had a sense of what to expect.

One of the central places that opened was Google's Campus London—a communal place for startups and investors and local ecosystem folks, located in the Shoreditch area of London, which was, at the time, an up-and-coming neighborhood. At first glance, it seemed rather desolate to me. Campus helped ignite the entire area, luring VCs (who eventually migrated over from Mayfair) and creative agencies and corporates who set up satellite offices there.

Eze Vidra, the head of Campus London, invited me over for a tour before the space officially opened, and we visited with Reshma Sohoni—the co-founder of Seedcamp, a European accelerator and venture capital firm—who had just moved in as an early resident.

It was a great moment in time where most anyone who was building or supporting startups could utilize Campus, but at the same time, it was a tight-knit community of people going against the grain.

It felt like London was starting to become the next NYC or Silicon Valley—there was a real sense of hope and optimism. Then the government started to pitch in, kicking off an initiative called Tech City, consisting of government programs for startups coupled with incentive programs for investors. It was fun for me to have a few startups and some investing experience under my belt while I was living in London because I felt like I had something useful and unique to share with the community.

On the other hand, compared to New York, London felt quaint and neighborhood-y. Living in Notting Hill, I would barely see my friends who lived in neighborhoods like Chelsea or East London. It was just so far away, and in London, people tend to stick to their neighborhoods.

We'd spend Sunday afternoons at this pub called The Westbourne, watching one soccer game or another, chatting with all the people we knew there, and then head over to The

Cow, another favorite neighborhood spot, to eat mussels and drink cheap white wine.

I made a point of becoming friends with folks that were not from the US—most of my friends, if they weren't British, were Italian and Spanish, Indian and Pakistani, and from all across the Middle East. It was a really great, eclectic group. And even better, on long weekends, when friends would go home to wherever they were from, they would take me along, so I got to do that around-the-world trip in some form after all, spending weekends in Dubai and Oman and all sorts of other amazing places. It was interesting because even though I grew up in New York City, which is very diverse, I didn't have much exposure to Middle Eastern culture, so to me, the UK felt even more diverse, at least in the global sense, than NYC.

Thanksgiving was one particular time where I definitely missed being in the US and with family and friends. I did have a couple of American friends in London; in fact, I had one, Charley, a Georgetown educated lawyer/banker who lived right next door. We decided to throw a Thanksgiving feast at his flat—and it evolved into one of those events where it was first ten people, then thirty, and ultimately, it seemed like every American in a ten-mile radius showed up. Everyone brought Thanksgiving staples—potluck style—like mashed potatoes and pecan pie, and it turned into one of the most fun and celebratory holiday meals and parties that I can remember.

Of course, in London and in all of my world travels, there were many good moments where I felt patriotic and needed to be with my American friends. But for the most part, during my time there, I tried to live a little bit more locally and immerse myself more in the culture. Geography and borders are truly fungible in the world we founders—and funders—travel through and live in.

I can't write a book about entrepreneurship without spotlighting stories and traits that involve extreme courage and determination. I refer to this attitude as MOXIE—which is a crucial part of the Everywhere Mindset. The person who embodies Moxie is someone who's a real force of nature and holds a deep well of courage and determination and, in this context, self-belief. A secondary part of the Moxie characteristic is self-reliance; nothing is going to stop this persona, and they make things happen for themselves. People with Moxie are unique and sometimes seen as quirky outsiders, but they are also some of the toughest and grittiest.

MOXIE IN ACTION:

» *Bold is beautiful.* I'd booked a trip around the world, which showed moxie in and of itself; then I landed somewhere (and shortly thereafter, worked in a role) I had never foreseen. I embraced the unknown fully, and it opened so many doors for me. Had I continued with my original plan and taken the next leg of the around-the-world flight to South Africa, my career could have gone in an entirely different direction.

» *Outsiders bring something important to the table.* I was living and operating outside of my prescribed lane culturally (and professionally), but I ran with it—and though I might have occasionally been misunderstood, I also brought a whole new sensibility around startups and innovation to the BBC and to the London startup community.

» *Forgiveness not permission.* From my email access to putting up my own rogue website for Labs, I was bold and forged ahead, sometimes without worrying too much about the consequences; I knew they wouldn't be dire, and in fact, ended up adding to a lot of my success there.

ELIZABETH ROSSIELLO, FOUNDER OF AZA FINANCE

Elizabeth Rossiello is nothing short of a firebrand—and not only in the world of finance, where, over the last decade, she has stormed the gates. She is the human embodiment of Moxie. Growing up in Queens, New York, Elizabeth didn't know any women who weren't nurses or teachers. Her "rich aunt" was a head secretary and had her own pool of secretaries working under her. Growing up, given her love of foreign languages and the fact that she spoke three of them fluently by the time she graduated high school, Elizabeth figured she would perhaps work at the UN as a foreign-language secretary.

Today, she has three secretarial/administrative assistants working for her alone at her fintech company, AZA Finance.

But how, I wondered, did she get from point A to point B?

She laughingly told me, "My first international trip was from Queens to the Upper East Side," where she attended the elite Hunter High School (and whose wealthy surrounding neighborhood is so different from working-class Queens that it does feel like a different country).

Though Hunter is a public school (hence, no tuition), it requires a test for admissions, and only the tiniest percentage of applicants get in; it's basically the most coveted school in New York City, and it was an early influence on Elizabeth, opening doors to worlds she hadn't yet thought of exploring. This is obviously where her Everywhere Mindset took root.

Slowly, from the people around her, she started learning more about what was possible.

"Every time I learned about a new career or a new place or a new direction, I would apply and go and then achieve it," said Elizabeth. "And that was a model for the rest of my life. I had a lot of goals, and I would go achieve them, and then I'd say to myself, *Look, you thought about this two years ago, and now you're here.*"

"I was almost shameless about moving my goalpost forward for myself," she told me, adding, "And thinking about what's next, because I think about how far I've come already, and I'm always assuming there's something else out there that I haven't been exposed to yet."

I'd been following Elizabeth's story closely, as there are not many women running blockchain startups, and I was an early investor in the space (such as with Chainalysis in 2015, as you will hear more about in my interview with Jonathan Levin in Chapter 13) so I took a keen interest. When I started investing in Africa, she popped up again in my life, as many companies I was meeting in the fintech/payments space were involved with or adjacent to BitPesa (the original name for her company, which is now called AZA). Plus, I know a few AZA employees and even a board member, so when I finally met Elizabeth briefly at a conference, I felt like I knew her already.

She reminds me of a fearless superhero, leaping over problems or challenges in a single bound without looking back. I asked her where that drive—that ability—came from.

Very similar to the train trip I took with my grandmother across Europe when I was nine, Elizabeth took a European trip on the Eurorail with her own family, which became important in two ways for her: 1) She'd already grown tired of sleeping on the floor (no room in hotel room beds for the third child!) and therefore decided she needed to really make it in this world; and 2) After meeting her Italian cousins, who also had red hair and freckles, she said to herself, *Wow, they're me, but here.*

At that moment, Elizabeth's Everywhere Mindset fully flowered.

Things further accelerated when she dropped out of Bryn Mawr college after one year (though they paused for a moment when she ironically took a yearlong job as a secretary to earn some money, catching a glimpse of what life could've been and what she originally thought it would be), then decided to attend SUNY Buffalo and graduate in one year.

"I talked the dean into letting me do it—I think I did twenty-five credits in one year," she told me with a grin. "I had two friends. I just studied and did ballet and cooked asparagus for bewildered Buffalonians who were like, *Who the hell are you?*"

"And *that* is going to go on my cemetery headstone," she laughed.

Elizabeth moved abroad to finish up her last semester at the Bundestag (the German federal parliament), where she'd been admitted into an intensive program in politics, Italian, and German. "And then I didn't come back after my graduation," she told me, "And I really didn't come back mentally…ever."

As a fellow traveler, wanderer, explorer, adventurer, that stuck with me—some people are just meant to move, live in other cultures, and feel at home anywhere in the world. I could relate.

The next couple of years involved some more programs and degrees, all in various locations abroad, until Elizabeth landed in the Credit Suisse analyst program.

Then quickly, she left.

"I was doing a lot of research, and other people were taking my work and running with it," she told me. "I just didn't want to play that chess game anymore."

Elizabeth moved on to a job with Planet Reading, which was a joint venture between Jacques Attali, an intellectual in Paris, and Muhammad Yunus, who had just won the Nobel Peace Prize for microfinance.

"It has the word finance in it," she said, describing her thought process at the time. "I can figure this out."

Elizabeth and her new husband set off for Nairobi, planning to stay for a year; they stayed for seven and left with little kids (and a divorce). Along the way, Elizabeth left Planet Reading and started consulting for various development agencies, where she built up vast expertise in microfinance.

Africa was also her entry into entrepreneurship, since she was surrounded by (male) friends who were founding companies and constantly asking her for a "quick chat" about microfinance. She found herself too many times cooking them dinner and giving them valuable research or market intel, which they ate up along with her gourmet chicken.

After sharing everything she knew, which was a *lot*, she'd ask about working at their companies, but they'd laugh and say, "No—you're pregnant!"

Then came a job opportunity at the International Finance Corporation (IFC), for which both Elizabeth and her husband—two years younger and far less knowledgeable and experienced in banking and finance—were candidates.

She told me, still incredulous after all these years, that they asked her point blank, "You have kids?"

She responded, "Yes. And so does he. They're the *same kids!*"

Her husband got the job.

After realizing then and there that life wasn't fair—especially for women with their burden of household and emotional labor, on top of making a living as a professional—Elizabeth got busy taking control of her business trajectory and decided to start her own enterprise.

She met with a well-known Bitcoin investor who offered her an initial $50,000 seed round of funding.

"I learned about Bitcoin in all of two weeks," she told me with her characteristic cheeky, wide smile. "I launched BitPesa about a month later."

Things snowballed when Elizabeth's good friend from her mom group wrote a *Bloomberg* article on the new company, and it went viral. Suddenly, she was fielding calls from Bitcoin and blockchain rockstars like Barry Silbert, Charles Hoskinson, and Peter Smith, and off she went. Still, she insisted to anyone who would listen, "I'm not an entrepreneur. I don't think I have that bone in my body." Until a friend finally chastised her, saying, "There is no bone. You just do it, or you don't."

Couple that with feeling like she had no other options (working for sexist men just wasn't in the cards for her anymore), and Elizabeth found herself squarely on her journey to understanding she was deeply capable (in my opinion, of pretty much anything). This is something most women go through, even the ones who outwardly share her brand of Moxie.

It was also about really believing that she (and her work) was truly valuable. And even though she was a divorced, single mom of three little kids, her risk profile shot up. "I think about that a lot, about how my risk profile changed over the course of my life," Elizabeth told me, musing, "Or how I realized what it was."

分分

Her fintech company, now called AZA Finance, is a digital foreign exchange (often referred to as an FX), which converts a given currency to another, or to cryptocurrency, optimizing that financial transaction and taking a cut of it. The risk component is that there's a "float": currency fluctuates and can be volatile in nature. AZA Finance supports upward of a hundred currencies and comprises a major part of the nucleus of international business, connecting accounts globally.

I've invested in fintech for years, and I can still get overwhelmed by the vastness and complexity of that (still largely uncharted) world. I asked Elizabeth how she navigated it.

She replied with her characteristic spunk: "It might be because I love languages and I've lived all over the world, but I thought, *You can't fool me with this blockchain stuff. This isn't that complex, and none of you really know what you're talking about. I call bullshit.*" She continued, "I heard a lot of people saying things at conferences that I knew technically weren't true, and definitely when they started talking about mobile money and P2P [peer-to-peer] payment processing, I was the expert. So, I think that encouraged me. Also, I was a mom. I haven't slept. I've got no fucks to give at this point, for sure."

Which led to Elizabeth plowing ahead even amidst a full eight years of struggle. [Side note: are you sensing a theme among all of the founders in this book?]

"It's this perpetual motion of, *I don't have other options. This has to work,*" Elizabeth said. "And not everybody has that feeling. Especially if you've done a big cash raise, you think, *I have options.*"

She added, "When you think it *has* to work, you do perform the best."

AZA kept iterating and recreating itself in the face of everything that came at them, including market forces or its business relationship with the infamous crypto founder Sam Bankman-Fried (SBF as he's known colloquially) and his company FTX.

When AZA decided to raise its Series C round of funding, SBF sent a plane to come pick Elizabeth and her team up in London to bring them to his home office in the Bahamas. There, they discussed a partnership intended to help FTX expand in Africa, which meant the crypto exchange would go on to become a customer of the payments firm but not have any sort of ownership interest.

This distinction was crucial for Elizabeth and AZA. When everything in SBF's orbit very publicly blew up (and though the fallout did reach her company to some degree), it was far from fatal. "We said, *This isn't the end of us. We're not going to die with some scandal*," Elizabeth said. "We went to each regulator, to each client, and we brought them all back on."

Elizabeth isn't planning on wasting any more time. They did enough of that, she told me, in the early years, teaching other people. It's time, maybe for the *first* time, to focus inward and solely on the AZA brand.

"Growing up with a lot of adversity, there are two paths, and only one of them takes you forward, and that's a positive mindset. And I've spent time on the other path," she said. "Every day I think, *What do I need to do today?* To eat well, to train almost like an athlete, to make sure that I am here and problem-solving."

Forging ahead might be too mild a phrase to describe all Elizabeth has overcome, and her Moxie drove the resilience which has lead to her success.

KEY INSIGHTS:
ELIZABETH AS A FOUNDER WITH MOXIE

» *Unapologetic (especially about herself).* Her powerful statement—"I was shameless about moving the goalpost forward for myself"—led to her equally powerful determination to succeed in business as one of the only women running a blockchain startup.

» *Resilience and relentlessness are closely related.* She faced hardships, lost out on job opportunities because she was a woman, carried her company through the FTX scandal, and raised three young children in a very foreign place after a divorce, but she still thrived in every way.

» ***Be a force for good.*** Elizabeth drove positive change in a forceful way. While she could have stayed in NYC and ended up a business consultant or on Wall Street, she chose to pursue a life of impact, which for her, meant building inclusive products and solutions for people in developing countries.

CHAPTER 4

AUSTRALIA

My role at the BBC took me to lots of places, and a favorite might be Australia, where I spent a large chunk of time immersed in the business culture, as well as soaking up that chill Aussie lifestyle, which was nothing short of a revelation for the Type-A New Yorker in me.

A few years prior to me joining, BBC Worldwide had excitedly acquired the travel guidebook publisher, *Lonely Planet*, but by the time I arrived at the company, everyone was in a panic wondering what to do with it. Lonely Planet was an iconic brand, much beloved by travelers around the world (including me), but the book publishing world was changing rapidly and dramatically into our new digital reality.

While struggling on the publishing side, the team at Lonely Planet had made a huge effort to innovate, think creatively, and get ahead of all of the changes on the digital front. One such experiment was a concept around a new combination mobile/social/local spinout company, and that's how I found myself in Melbourne for a few weeks: I was there to help to get this initiative going and act as the interim CEO.

The CEO of Lonely Planet at the time, Matt Goldberg (who is now the CEO of TripAdvisor), was excited about this project and assembled a lively cast of characters to help get it going, with buy-in from all the business unit owners at Lonely

Planet who would need to collaborate on the content, tech, legal, and distribution sides.

This was a true on-the-ground experience in Australia, and I arrived poised to do big things. Since this was an internal "incubation," my first task was to solidify the team and ensure they had the right DNA for the leadership and execution abilities needed for eventually spinning out into an independent company.

Just like I did when I started Labs, which I detailed in the previous chapter, I spent my days meeting as many people as I could at Lonely Planet and kicking the tires—making sure they were road-ready while bearing in mind the road may be filled with potholes—on any potential founding team members.

Lonely Planet resembled a startup from the outside with a cool office vibe and a plethora of hard-working, incredibly smart people. But one thing it *didn't* have was a ton of people with an appetite for risk. Historically, Australia's financial culture was quite conservative, with people mostly prioritizing stability, saving for retirement, and buying property, rather than investing in volatile assets. Similarly (and unlike many traditional startup founders and teams), this crew didn't really want to give up their stable salaries and variety of benefits. Because of that, I wasn't sure how the economics were going to work. So, I just squinted, ignored everything I'd learned running my own startup—things like running a super lean organization pre-product market fit, shipping early and often, and having the majority of the founders working for equity rather than a healthy salary—and hoped for the best.

Their relative fiscal conservatism didn't impact the startup ethos in Australia, though, which was all about going global— thinking big—from day one, albeit doing it in a more capital-efficient way. In part, that's because it's a relatively small country (and certainly geographically isolated), which is also why Australians are great at building bridges between people, countries, and cultures—a big part of the Everywhere Mindset. It's out of necessity.

The 1990s put Australia on the software startup map after the dot-com boom with the creation of companies like Seek and realestate.com.au, and by the early 2000s, US-based companies like Microsoft, Google, and AWS began opening offices in Sydney, drawn to the ease of the shared language (English) and the fact that the country was a gateway to Asia. That created the foundation for later well-known platforms like Atlassian and Canva (Atlassian went public on NASDAQ, and Canva is currently a decacorn; both are headquartered in Australia), as well as Employment Hero, Dovetail, SafetyCulture, LinkTree, and Culture Amp, among others.

Another interesting component to the Australian startup environment is the government support behind it; that in and of itself isn't rare—a lot of countries offer incentives for startups (see my chapter on Dubai/Saudi Arabia for another example of this), but Australia is a special case. Its government wants the tech sector to significantly contribute to its GDP, and for 1.2 million people to be landed in tech jobs by 2030.

At that moment, under the auspices of Lonely Planet's spinout, and then later as a VC, that made my ears perk up and kept my focus on Australia as a real land of opportunity in coming years.

৭৬

I made sure that my time in the beautiful country of Australia wasn't all work and carved out time to have fun, which for me, of course, always means exploration and travel.

While most people love Sydney, it's Melbourne (and greater Victoria state) that really spoke to me; the people, the natural beauty, and the vibe all felt like Northern California, both familiar and comforting, yet also outside of my normal state of being.

While I was there for an extended period working from the Lonely Planet office, I got to know my way around. One long weekend, I rented a car solo and drove the Great Ocean Road (trying to get accustomed to driving stick shift on the opposite side of the road was only slightly terrifying), which looks much like Big Sur with limestone cliffs, world-class surfing breaks, and charming seaside towns—but with some differences, of course, like koala-filled eucalyptus trees.

The problem when I embarked on that getaway was that I hadn't realized it was a holiday weekend—I'd assumed I'd be able to just pull over and get a hotel room anywhere along the way. No such luck. The place was fully booked months in advance, and I was totally stuck.

Contemplating sleeping in the car, which seemed like my only real option, I ducked into a super cute hippie cafe in Apollo Bay to distract myself with a kombucha.

I started talking to the woman behind the counter who was making the wraps and serving up delicious scones. She resignedly shook her head when I asked her if there were any nearby places to stay.

But after a few more minutes of chatting (and her picking up from my accent that I was not from around there), she lit up when I told her that I lived in New York, a place she'd always wanted to visit. Next thing I know, she's making calls, and a few minutes later a guy, his daughter, and their dog walk into the store and offer to put me up in their attic down the road.

And that's how I came to love the Great Ocean Road, the state of Victoria, and the local people. I stayed for a few days since Apollo was a good base to visit the majestic limestone structures of the Twelve Apostles in the Port Campbell

National Park and observe the little penguins as they waddled back to shore.

It's also a reminder that people are, worldwide, really wonderful—and while traveling can sometimes bring some stress and discomfort, it's also an opportunity to stretch my wings, leading me to fly to some amazing places. Welcome to the Everywhere Mindset.

゚゚゚゚

But then it was back down to earth and reality at the Lonely Planet office and the spinout company, where it started to feel like I was spinning my wheels trying to bring it to life.

Ultimately, it didn't work. We couldn't find a product/market fit nor a sustainable business model, and the company was rolled back into the parent company.

My biggest lesson here, which has informed my investment philosophy to this day (outside of the fact that spin-outs are just hard!), is that, at the early stage, you need a passionate group of founders who own the majority of the company. Hiring a team and creating a "Frankenstein" company is very difficult to get right. Although a small group of venture studios have been successful, more often than not, it's not a sustainable model.

But that wasn't the end of my Australian adventure.

Years later, in 2020 during the height of lockdown, Mark Finn, the co-founder and CFO of ROLLER, and the founder I spotlight as part of this chapter, called me. He'd been following the Everywhere Ventures story and wanted to get more involved, so he asked me to consider launching an offshoot of our fund in Australia. Although we were on a tear of expansion—LA and London were our first growth areas outside of NYC—Australia felt a bit farther afield.

But Mark was persistent and made the following arguments: (1) Australia was underserved at the pre-seed stage, with most investors getting involved at the time of product/market fit; (2) Australia had produced some great startup successes like Atlassian, Canva, and Afterpay—which were, by then, household names—and those founders and early employees were starting new companies; and (3) He would help me.

That sealed the deal for me, and the next thing I know, I'm calling our fund lawyers and back-office staff and spending evenings working on a limited partner agreement (LPA)—the document that limited partners and general partners sign outlining the rights and responsibilities of each group.

To pull this off, we needed to get the right investment team in place (sadly, Mark was tied up with ROLLER so he couldn't join us), but we found a great group of founders and operators with investment experience to join us on the investment committee, and Mark helped us rally some of our local backers.

Once we launched, I was shocked to join the weekly investment committee meeting on Zoom and still see everyone over there, all of whom were under a strict COVID lockdown. While things were definitely not great in the US, we had the freedom to leave our homes, go to the grocery store, and enjoy the parks. That was not the case in parts of Australia where the lockdown was much more severe.

Over the next eighteen months, we saw them in and out of lockdown and mostly in the same spot we left them the previous week, in sweatpants and on their sofas. It was hard to witness but also spoke to the culture there: while Americans would have been rioting, citing violations of personal freedom, Australians tend to focus on the greater good of the community, and they complied with the regulations without too much fuss. I finally got to see the super chill Australian stereotype in action, taking everything in stride.

Not everything has been easy, of course—it's a struggle for me to make the 9:00 p.m. Eastern time investment committee calls each week (I'm an early-morning person), and the founder community has different needs than those in the US. So, we continue to iterate our model and make tweaks based on the local needs.

But it's paying off—we've been able to build a footprint in the region and invest in several impactful founders building the future of healthcare, climate, insurance, and beyond.

An ELASTIC person is one who is flexible, adaptable, and resilient—all key elements of the Everywhere Mindset and those that embody it. Even as life throws curveballs, the Elastic can often catch them, nimbly adjusting to changing circumstances and taking on unexpected challenges without getting too ruffled. When faced with adversity, Elastics bounce back quickly and typically adopt a positive attitude about the experience as a whole. They are curious and willing to explore new concepts and approaches, which helps them navigate varying social and professional situations—they usually have growth/learning mindsets. I have a soft spot for Elastics because they are both self-aware and empathetic and can manage their own emotions effectively while understanding the feelings and motivations of those around them. The Elastic person is also creative and versatile, finding solutions to complex problems by leveraging their adaptability and resourcefulness.

ELASTIC IN ACTION:

> » *Reframe challenges into opportunities.* When Mark Finn asked us to consider launching our Everywhere Ventures fund in Australia, I had my reservations, thinking it was a distraction from our core thesis (and

a somewhat crazy move for a micro-fund based in NYC). But as we learned more and talked to the right people, we decided to pursue it, carving out a fitting opportunity in that area for us.

» ***Go with the Flow.*** When I was building the Lonely Planet spinout company, my instincts told me to do one thing but instead, I made the decision to go with the flow for the greater good while I gathered data and built allies. This was not easy for me as someone who has strong opinions and a strong inner voice, but ultimately, understanding the culture and the big picture of the organization was helpful to succeed in the role and effect long-term change.

» ***Pause—but then move.*** When I found myself stranded without a hotel on Great Ocean Road, I could've cut my losses, turned around, and driven back to where I was staying. Instead, I took stock of my situation and took the next right action, which ended up offering me the experience I was seeking…and the perfect place to stay!

MARK FINN, CO-FOUNDER OF ROLLER

Like many of the founders in *Venture Everywhere*, Mark Finn embodies multiple nationalities—he was born in the UK, lived in New Zealand, then Brisbane, Australia, then New Zealand again, and back to Melbourne, Australia, all by the time he was twelve years old. And that's not counting the time he spent in later years in Europe and New York City before ultimately settling down in Australia as an adult.

Naturally embracing the Everywhere Mindset? Absolutely. But as the saying goes, all politics (or in his case, business) is local. For Mark this is especially true because his nuclear family has been intrinsic to his and ROLLER's success, and that permeated our entire conversation.

Given the deep importance of community to Mark, it's fitting that ROLLER is a venue-managing software for in-person events (from small businesses like trampoline parks up to large arenas), made so that their operators can more seamlessly offer amazing places for people to gather and incredible experiences once they're there, while offering venues a "whole-of-business" solution to help them grow.

He started the company with his brother, Luke, and he readily admits the support of his parents not only helped plant their ambition (never pressuring them to work a more traditional path even after they graduated university with more traditional degrees), but they also always offered "a couch to sleep on"—which became their platform to take the big risk of becoming founders.

It was, he told me with a fond smile, "Ambition with a backstop."

৭৬

Long before we sat down in 2024 for this interview, Mark walked into my Techstars office one day back in 2015 with a crew of five other PricewaterhouseCoopers consultants. The PwC folks were interested in getting closer to startups and better understanding how PwC could work with early-stage companies.

Sitting around the conference room table, Mark and his colleagues grilled me on everything related to the accelerator program, firing questions at me as only consultants can. At the end of the session, as they were milling around the office talking to the various startup founders, Mark and I started chatting. His warmth and down-to-earth nature was apparent, and he had a curiosity in his eye that I didn't sense from the others—a genuine interest in my work and empathy for the founders I was working with. When he asked to come back the following week to jam on some other ideas, I told him he was more than welcome. By the second visit, I had sniffed him out, learning that Mark had founded ROLLER with his brother but had taken a break from his business to make some money and develop relationships around the world, which is why he was working at PwC.

So much about almost every founder's journey is non-linear; there's no rocket that transports anyone from zero to successful startup, and I could relate to him on that level too.

From there, Mark and I became fast friends, and I always enjoyed talking about tech trends and introducing him to other startups to bolster his corporate work, but I knew his heart was always with ROLLER. So, in 2019, when he told me he was moving back to Australia after four years in NYC to focus on ROLLER full time, I was sad but not surprised.

Our friendship and entrepreneurial story wouldn't end there, though. When he moved back to Australia, Mark was excited about all the changes he saw on the ground, with the massive successes of a few startups like Atlassian and Canva, which were helping to kick-start the entire startup community and changing the narrative about what was possible.

🐦🐦

By the time he moved back to resume building ROLLER in 2019, Mark had been walking through the fire with his company for nearly a decade. He and Luke had founded it in 2010, but at the time, there was no real investor ecosystem in Australia to speak of.

"There was no one you'd exactly call a sophisticated angel," Mark said with a smile. And their company had scant funding, which leads to when I met Mark in 2015. He'd taken the job at PwC to help cash-flow ROLLER while Luke stayed in Oz to keep things afloat operationally.

I can't emphasize enough how inspiring it has been to me and others to witness Mark's journey; it's the best demonstration of the long game I've seen yet. They've been at this for *fourteen years* and only turned the corner in the last couple of years. Taking on a side gig (and a very intense one at that) so his company could live to see another day is next-level.

I had to ask Mark where that resilience and grit—and entrepreneurial spirit—came from.

As is the case with many parts of Mark's story, this, too, started with his family. His dad had a corporate career but was entrepreneurial in the sense that, according to Mark, "He moved into different roles and went from one industry to another and had a global perspective. He had this unique ability to make other people believe in his companies and that anything was possible. And I think that rubbed off a lot on us being around him."

Mark told me in that paradigm, his dad was exposed to founders and inspired by them, so when his sons decided to go down that path, he encouraged them to "pursue things, and pursue them early."

The other aspect of the elasticity I uncovered was a distinct part of Mark and Luke's *own* belief in what they were building, which Mark ascribes to a few things. One of which is their brotherly bond and partnership: they bolstered each other if one or the other wavered. But he also told me they're both musicians and play together, and he believed that same creativity and harmony flowed into their business life as well. Flow is the operative word here, as founders, not unlike artists or musicians, do have to be process-oriented and organized but they often also let in creativity and flexibility to polish what they created to a shine.

Fittingly, in the middle of our conversation, Mark quoted a song lyric from a famous musician that referenced not needing any guide, since [he] "already knew the way."

In *that* way, he and Luke simply kept going. Or surviving, as Mark said. "We made a ton of mistakes. Experience is the worst teacher because you learn the lesson after the fact," he told me with a laugh, shaking his head. "You have to go through the fire to learn…and we just made it work, one way or another. We were scrappy, and it was messy."

Things got even messier for ROLLER—which is, remember, a *live events* software company—when COVID hit. "We had many near-death experiences," Mark told me matter-of-factly, and the pandemic was one of them.

A few years prior, fundraising had been another one. They'd gained some traction with their business and financials and had built a team of around twenty-five people, so they decided to raise a round of capital.

And were promptly rejected by the upwards of fifty investors they approached.

At this point in our talk, Mark got teary-eyed with emotion before telling me that once again, his family stepped in with support. His parents were the ones—with their deep belief in the company and their sons—who invested additional capital to keep ROLLER going and help it begin its ascent to the next level. Sometimes the "Everywhere" can be in your own backyard.

"You have these true tests where you're in the Indiana Jones moment of, *what do you really believe?*" Mark mused. "And then, you just have to. We had to make it work, and there was just no way that we weren't going to make it work."

Mark, of course, had a built-in support system in his brother and co-founder. But unlike many founders, they also felt that they had time. Mark (and Luke) gave themselves, as he described it, "The oxygen to find the thing that is the thing."

In discussing the company's slower growth trajectory with Mark, I was reminded of the time I had dinner with him and Luke at Gemma restaurant in the Bowery Hotel in NYC. They were in town meeting with some of the firms who were interested in leading their funding round, and they asked my opinion about all of them. Without hesitation, I advised them to look closely at Insight Partners (even though, at the time, they were leaning towards other firms).

I didn't hear from them for a few weeks, then learned they had signed with Insight, raising $50 million in growth capital to further enhance their platform and services.

It was such a statement on Mark's elasticity and ability to stay open-minded when presented with data, but overall, their story is also so moving to me in its longevity—it flies in the face of the whole "fail fast" invocation I hear so often in the startup world. In the case of ROLLER, it was a slow burn.

KEY INSIGHTS: MARK AS AN ELASTIC FOUNDER

» *Embrace the moment.* Or more aptly, embrace the "Indiana Jones moment" as Mark called it. Whatever is happening at a given time—especially the messiness and mistakes—is valuable. Mark admitted they made a "ton" of mistakes (and like every founder, probably still make them along the way), but they all were significant in fostering their ultimate success and longevity.

» *The best path forward will likely not be a straight line.* Moving to NYC and working at PwC in the middle of building their company may not have seemed like the most obvious way to move it forward, but it did just that, helping support the business. Mark also had an amazing few years in NYC, which broadened his network and his thinking more generally, creating that twelve-year (and counting) "overnight" success story he's living!

» ***Things are not always what they seem.*** The most obvious example of this is that Mark was working as a PwC consultant at one point but was actually a startup founder. More broadly, it's important to remember that you never know what a person's backstory is and what they're bringing to the table.

CHAPTER 5

SPAIN

I went to visit Barcelona for a weekend but stayed for a year. I'd been living in London, working for the BBC, and travel was part of my job. I was always on the road, and no one at the company ever knew where I was dialing in from. I was an early "global nomad," working remotely and traveling (Everywhere, of course) with my laptop in tow.

I'd arrived in London in the winter, fell in love with it, and then "June Gloom" hit. I was decidedly unprepared. I assumed I'd be wearing shorts and summer dresses like I did in New York, but London was relentlessly rainy and cold. One early summer day, we still had the heat on.

I started to cry.

I called my good friend Anna, whom I'd met on a flight to Spain when I was on my way to the Mobile World Congress Conference. I was speaking at said conference and wanted to be rested, so as we took off, I took a sleeping pill. That's something I don't normally do, and that little pill knocked me out cold. During the trip, there was a huge storm. We were rocking through the worst turbulence, the woman next to me (Anna, still a stranger, but not for long) was freaking out, and I was none the wiser.

I came to just as a voice boomed over the loudspeaker, "Welcome to Paris!"

The problem was, my conference was in Barcelona; the flight had been diverted because of the storm. Anna and I became fast friends over the next twenty-four hours as she helped me scramble to get rerouted—via literal planes, trains, and automobiles since there were no flight options for days—to be able to make it to the stage for my keynote.

Two years later, as I looked forlornly out the window of my London apartment and complained bitterly to her about the weather, Anna said, "Come to Barcelona and visit me—it will be great!"

Staying in that city wasn't some major life decision I came to.

For me, hard work was always equated with long hours grinding in an office—as I've described, I came from the worlds of law and finance in New York City, where that kind of life is the gold standard. That aforementioned global nomad life—still working hard, but at cafes and in beautiful places surrounded by cool people—didn't come naturally to me, to say the least.

During my trip to Barcelona, Anna and I went to a party at my Swedish friend Magnus's new flat in the gothic quarter—it was right near the water with a huge terrace. His company, Golden Gecko, was an app development company and a rather successful early player in the mobile app space, and he had built it from scratch in Barcelona, far away from the traditional life his other friends and family were living in Stockholm.

As we stood on his balcony sipping drinks and gazing out over the water that balmy evening, Magnus turned to me and said, "You know, Jenny, it's possible to do great work and be successful but *also* have a life."

It was the first time anyone had ever said anything like that to me, and it hit me to my core. I decided to stay in Barcelona and try it out and notch my own Everywhere Mindset up a few levels.

Even better, the store Zara is based in Spain, and I happened to be there right when they held their bi-annual blowout sale—what else did I need? I'm a minimalist anyway, having gotten used to traveling around the world for months at a time with only the smallest roller bag, so I didn't need much: a few sundresses and I was set.

From there, things just started falling into place. My friend in New York knew an Italian woman who needed to sublet her apartment in Barcelona's Old Quarter in the El Born neighborhood. I was stunned when I saw it, especially looking out the window at the Santa Caterina Market—the roof below was mesmerizing, made of waves of colors and intricate tiling. Some of it is noticeable from street level or when walking through the market, but living above it gave me a rare bird's-eye—and beautiful—view.

My fascination with Barcelona (or "Barca" as locals call it) started, as many of my adventures did, with my grandma. When I was younger, she and I took a number of trips there, starting our mornings at La Boqueria eating *jamon* (yes, for breakfast!) and getting lost in the market, weaving in and out of stalls stuffed with all sorts of fantastic—and fantastical, at least to me—items.

I've loved olives since childhood, so I was delighted when I learned on one of our visits to Barca that La Boqueria had an amazing olive stand. I used to go to it every day while my grandma was off negotiating the price of spices or fruit a few stalls away.

I asked to try each and every olive (they had thirty-plus types) before deciding which to buy. I was young and cute, and the guy running the stand would humor me, carefully placing each type of olive in my hand until I was stuffed. Then I'd just tell him that *he* could pick the ones we should buy, and my grandma would end up giving them away to the guys hanging out on Las Ramblas, the famous street in central Barcelona.

When I lived there all those years later, the very same man was selling olives. He didn't remember me (although he pretended to), but it was another reason the city felt so close to my heart.

Grandma and I also visited Park Guell, one of the largest green spaces in Barcelona, named after the famous architect and designer Antoni Gaudi, whose fingerprints are all over Barcelona; she loved his colors and patterns and surreal lines.

We spent hours roaming the old city of Gracia looking for a hat maker whom my grandma had heard about. When we finally found him, he didn't speak a word of English, but somehow, she was able to relay her desire for a Cordovan hat, embellished with red tassels and ribbons. Personally, I always thought it looked like a lamp shade, but she loved that hat and proudly wore it back in Brooklyn.

One of my grandma's sisters, Gertie, was also obsessed with Spain and exclusively wore Spanish-style dresses, sky-high platform shoes, and dyed her hair jet-black. She kept a pair of castanets in her purse at all times just in case she needed to break into flamenco dance at any moment, however unlikely such an emergency might be in Forest Hills, Queens, where she lived. There were endless weekends at her house spent learning about Spanish culture, eating her version of *tortilla Espanola*, trying on outfits in her attic, and patiently viewing two-hour slideshows of her and my great uncle Max's Spanish adventures. When Gertie died, we buried her with her castanets in her casket.

Needless to say, by the time I arrived in Barcelona, I already felt like a local.

The apartment I'd found over the Market was in a cute little walkup building with no attendant in the lobby.

Right downstairs, there was a bodega called Maxis where you could buy drinks, phone cards, snacks, and other little necessities. It was run by another group of non-locals (noticeable since they were speaking English and not Spanish or Catalan)—Nigerians—who would hang out in front of the store telling stories, watching soccer on a TV they'd dragged into the street, and generally talking fast and joking around.

When I first moved in and would walk by them after a night out, they'd whistle at me, cat-call, and say things like, "Psssst. Hey girl, what's shakin'?"

It wasn't threatening, only annoying, but on my third night in my new apartment, I made a decision. I stopped squarely in front of the six guys, looked them straight in the face and said, "Hey, I'm Jenny. I live upstairs, I'm from New York City, and you can either cat-call me every night, or we can just be friends."

After some hooting and hollering at my boldness and lots of fist bumps all around, those guys instantly became my neighborhood crew, stand-in doormen (holding my FedEx packages for me when they arrived), bouncers, protectors, and friends.

Friends would come by my place to see me, and they'd tell them, "Oh, yeah, Jenny's out, but she'll be back at 4:00." When guys I was dating stopped over, they'd say, "You better be on your best behavior; we'll be watching from downstairs."

There was something about the fact that we were all foreigners in Spain—none of us spoke the local Catalan language, and we were all outsiders of sorts—that really bonded us. The Everywhere Mindset can be broad and wide, but much like we humans, it consists of connective tissue. I reveled in those nights with them, hanging out on the stoop watching soccer, drinking Fanta, and chatting.

Barcelona has a terrible problem with petty crime and pick-pockets, and we lived near a tourist area, which compounded that exponentially. We'd be sitting outside the bodega, which was situated down a small alley, and tourists would sit out-side at nearby cafes and put their phones on the table, totally exposed, as they may have been used to doing back in Texas or Colorado.

Like clockwork, in the evenings, we'd hear *thump, thump, thump.*

The Maxis guys and I would just look at each other know-ingly, saying, "Oh, there goes another phone."

And then in a flash, we'd see the guy who took the phone fly by us on his bike. Seconds later, a much more slow-moving American tourist wearing sandals and socks would run past, screaming after them.

And that's what it's really like being a part of the true fab-ric of any given place—you accept it and love it, flaws and all.

One morning, I was sipping tea in my apartment and heard all kinds of yelling on the street. Alarmed, I ran to the balcony and looked down over the market, where I was amazed to see thousands of people marching with flags and shouting in Catalan.

My neighborhood was a funny melting pot, and there would be protests like this all the time: people flooding the streets, shaking flags, yelling, and rallying. I was never entirely sure what they were protesting about (though it usually was underpinned by calls for Catalan independence or better working conditions), but they were super passionate, never violent, and they took breaks from protesting during the sum-mer holidays, which was so polite!

But at that moment, I realized that not only was Barcelona a place of incredible beauty, amazing food, and charming beach life, but it was also a place with a complex social structure dating back hundreds of years.

Sometimes Europe seems like a make-believe wonderland to Americans because we don't have cities anywhere near as old and as beautiful in the US. But when you hear the yelling and see the anger in protesters' faces, you remember that everything is not as it seems to the tourists, and there is a lot of nuance within Spain—and everywhere else—that many of us from other places may never understand.

🐦🐦

Home is a feeling, far bigger than the physical walls of a dwelling or the borders of a geographical enclave. And for me, relationships are everything, so though Barca wasn't going to be my permanent home, the friends I made and the people I met made me *feel* like I was right where I belonged.

There were a lot of people there like me who worked in tech or on startups, and it all unfolded naturally: one person introduced me to another person, and within a couple of weeks, I had a really good crew of friends.

One of my first friends in Barcelona was a British guy named Jonathan who lived on a boat in the harbor. One Friday afternoon he invited me out for a sail. After a few hours of strenuously sailing (it was just the two of us on the boat), I looked out at the open water and asked, "Where exactly are we going, Jonathan?"

"Formentera!" he proclaimed.

Seeing that it was a two-day sail and I only had the clothes on my back and had to show up to work on Monday morning, I'm shocked I didn't blink. I told you I had ratcheted up my Everywhere Mindset!

Growing up, my parents were definitely *not* digital nomads, and the idea of traveling while working was foreign to them. You were either working at the office or on vacation, but definitely not both at the same time.

By that time, though, I'd learned that was how people in Barcelona rolled. Life was different there than it was in New York, and it meant working to live, not living to work—and most importantly, living for today.

In Barcelona, it was very hard to meet or become good friends with locals because Catalan is a difficult language to grasp for non-native speakers. Because of that, expats are a little bit more alienated than they would be in other places where it's easier and more practical to learn the language, and the international community in Barca is very tight knit, so it became an instant community for me.

I went out to big dinners with ten or twelve expats, from all different places (there were Italians, some Germans, lots of Scandinavians, and more), but everyone spoke English because it was and is the universal language for mutual understanding. It was funny to gaze around the table and realize I was the only native English speaker there.

(In my company, which invests in and works with founders all over the globe, there's one common denominator—they're all determined to learn English. Now, much of the tech-focused programming at every business event I go to anywhere in the world is in English.)

I also can't emphasize enough the late-night aspect of Spanish culture. The night is still *young* at 10:00 or 11:00 p.m., when most dinners in Barcelona are taking place (even on a Monday or Tuesday) and when most Americans are curled up watching Netflix or already asleep.

Inexplicably—at least to me in those early days in Barca—the happy-hour scene is also thriving, with everyone going out for Cava—Spanish champagne—after work.

When I drink, I tend to be a lightweight. I'd meet my new friends at around 6:00 p.m., and, getting into the spirit of things, start sipping with everyone else. As I said, though, dinner wasn't until later at night, and in Barcelona, you honestly can't get an ounce of food before nine, because only then is when the restaurants open for dinner.

One friend would be calling around for a reservation for ten people later that night, and someone would inevitably say, "No, we only need it for nine, because there's no way Jenny's going to make it."

I would have my two or so glasses of Cava on an empty stomach at a place called El Xampanyet down the street from where I lived. Laughing and tipsy, my group would walk me home, where I'd promptly fall asleep at 8:30, never making it to dinner in Barca and always waking up famished (thank goodness for churros con chocolate), only to begin again the next evening after work.

❧❧

I may not have been much of a drinker, but I found other ways to settle in deeper in Barcelona, particularly within the emerging startup culture there.

Before I moved there, the city had done a lot in the prior decade to revitalize an old industrial area called El Poblenou and turn it into a successful tech/biotech/business hub for the city. This project became the blueprint worldwide for "innovation districts"—concentrated hubs of business that are very accessible and include a mix of office space, housing, and other amenities.

At the time, there was a lot of excitement about the next phase of that development, which meant attracting international companies. In 2008, Yahoo made Barcelona their international headquarters, and expats flooded in.

However, after the Global Financial Crisis, when I lived in Barca, it felt like the city was at a crossroads, still trying to attract tech expats like me but not exactly making it easy to set up shop (literally and figuratively) there. It took me a *full three months* to get my Wi-Fi set up. Getting a work visa was almost impossible, so I officially came and went for the year that I stayed there as a "tourist," a pretty common practice among expats. (If you are reading this and work in Immigration and Border Control in Spain, please know this book is a work of fiction.)

But snail-like bureaucracy didn't stop people from coming to the city. One thing I realized while living in Barcelona is that many of the entrepreneurs I met were from elsewhere in Europe but living there for the amazing lifestyle: incredible food, city beaches, cheaper cost of living than where they came from, and that "work-to-live" mentality I described earlier. The Swedes and Germans were escaping the brutal weather, the British were loving the currency arbitrage, and the French were just escaping other French!

Early on in my stint in Barca, I was introduced to handsome, Ken-doll-esque identical twins, Holger and Henrik, who'd fled the bad weather and their more traditional lives in Germany (if both of them holding PhDs and MBAs can be described as "traditional") to set up business and life in Barcelona.

Together, they had a gift for spotting "white spaces" before others and filling the gap, something we now refer to as a "startup studio," in which a group of innovators come up with a bunch of ideas and then build companies around these ideas. Instead of starting just one company, they spin up a bunch of companies at once, recruit a team to run each venture, and surround the venture with resources and cash. Venture studios are very popular now, but back around 2010, the brothers were ahead of their time, especially in Europe. Some of the companies Holger and Henrik helped incubate— and that I loyally patronized—included a scooter company called Cooltra and Asian fusion fast-food restaurants they set up all over town, among other tech, media, and health-focused companies.

One day, I stopped by their office in the Eixample neighborhood to visit. In the entryway, there was a massive whiteboard (a word that has since become a verb) that listed more than seventy ideas they were contemplating for new startups. I stopped and stared, impressed.

At that point, Barcelona was like a startup wonderland for me. The twins and people like them could see the city with fresh eyes, clearly envisioning the future of the city (and the world) and where the opportunities were.

Although I was a founder myself, I was more of an empath, really wanting to solve problems that I personally felt and/or experienced in my immediate sphere. But this was an entirely different kind of entrepreneurship, much more calculated and clinical...and my eyes were opened.

I had always thought that you had to first be passionate about the idea to start a company, but what I saw with the brothers' startup studio is that you can see things missing in the world and look to plug those holes. I call these types of founders the "MBAs" because they study the market opportunity and focus on maximizing business models similar to the way business school students do. For example, Barcelona didn't have an app-based scooter company when they started Cooltra, and the city was perfect for it; they may not have personally cared about scooters (or maybe they did!), but the point is, they *saw* the market before one existed.

Various types of founders can all be—and are—super successful in different contexts. In fact, context is key throughout the entire global startup ecosystem.

While living there, I was introduced to a Barcelona-based venture capital firm—it was the only one in town at the time—and they invited me into their office to meet the founding partners.

After the usual round of multiple kisses followed by espressos, I was struck by how different they were than the VCs I knew back home. Even though Barcelona, in some ways, was a more easy-going culture, here, the hoodies I was used to seeing in the Bay Area were replaced with monogrammed shirts, and sneakers were replaced with loafers. These guys came out of finance and big corporations, so this was their idea of casual. This was an interesting juxtaposition from the startup environment in the US, where increasingly, many investors came from operating and/or founder backgrounds (like me) and T-shirts and jeans were de rigueur.

Later, after traveling more—and expanding my portfolio and experience—I realized that, at the time I was living there, Spain didn't yet have the cohort of successful tech founders—the first generation—who would inevitably turn into angel investors. Compare that to Silicon Valley which had already had a *few* waves of this innovation flywheel going, like the famed "PayPal Mafia," which later seeded the founders of Facebook, AirBnb, and SpaceX.

As Spain didn't have those previous waves of successful founders, it was former finance and corporate people who raised the first venture capital funds, not other founders and operators. Although Spain has many of the raw ingredients of a thriving tech ecosystem (great engineering schools, corporates, capital), it takes some time for that wealth and intellectual capital to start to recycle into the next generation.

In a parallel example, the New York tech scene started with ad tech (all the analog advertising agencies morphed into digital), then moved into e-commerce (the multinational brands based in NYC went online), and has now moved into things like fintech (because NYC has all the banks). Similarly, the first iteration of Spanish tech startup was contextual to the local businesses—travel and hospitality—which of course made sense: Spain is the second most visited-by-tourists country in the world, and so much of the economy relies on tourism.

At the time, this meant the flourishing of consumer apps, and I had a front-row seat in Barcelona as founders were taking analog businesses (things like travel agencies, olive importing outfits, and language learning schools) and creating the digital versions of them. These have now evolved to other areas like last-mile delivery and mobility startups, showing how local context in business and startups could be parlayed into a global presence.

Ultimately, my time in Barcelona taught me *so* much—about both business and life—but most importantly, I learned how adaptable I can be. I moved there without planning to move, never looking back or overthinking it (things weren't perfect in London at the time, so I simply worked my way into a better situation in Barcelona quickly). I was able to fluidly context-switch from a rigid office worker to a Barcelona global nomad, and I did things like find the perfect housing and make a huge and disparate variety of new friends quickly despite only knowing one person there when I arrived. Before my time there, I wouldn't have necessarily considered myself as elastic, but now I see that the Everywhere Mindset was well-seeded inside of me, as well as in the entrepreneurs I observed and interacted with there.

This chapter is the second iteration of the ELASTIC component of the Everywhere Mindset and serves as an important reminder that Elastics are not flimsy or changing direction all the time; rather, they are able to read a given situation in that moment and adapt to what's required.

ELASTIC IN ACTION:

» ***Don't bring too much baggage.*** Yes, I'm a very light packer, which I recommend to anyone who wants to be able to move more freely around the world, but this applies more broadly too: I ended up moving to Barcelona more or less on a whim, and since I didn't overthink things, they started to fall into place for me there. I traveled light in every way, which meant I could glide more easily into the next opportunity.

» ***Set sail (safely).*** A short harbor sail on my friend Jonathan's boat turned into a weekend adventure to Formentera, a place I had never been, and with which I fell in love. This is another flow I just went with, but I also had some guardrails in place, by way of a trusted friend leading me on that journey.

» ***Today's foe might be tomorrow's friend.*** My Nigerian neighbors in Maxis bodega went from catcalling me to being my good buddies, which taught me an important lesson about taking the time to look people in the eye and getting to know who they really are. It's also about perspective and frame of mind—being open to the people who cross your path from all walks of life.

KIRILL BIGAI, CO-FOUNDER OF PREPLY

Kirill's grounded and thoughtful demeanor belies everything he has gone through as a founder—not just with his company's ups and downs, but also in the broader geopolitical climate with a front-row seat to revolution and war.

In the middle of our conversation, as Kirill was describing the start of the Russian invasion in his home country of Ukraine and the ensuing chaos there, he got choked up.

"I'm sorry," he said. "I didn't expect to get this emotional."

After a brief pause, he continued his story. As soon as he got the news that the war had begun, he knew he had to immediately act. However, he said, "It was almost mission impossible. Because within a day in Kyiv, there were no buses, there were no cars, there was no petrol. There was nothing. There was no means to leave Kyiv at all."

But he wasted no time in setting up a ten-person team that worked around the clock for two weeks providing logistics, financial, legal, and mental health support for the 150 "Preplers" in Kyiv, many of whom were young foreigners and expats who didn't have anyone else there to rely on and didn't speak Ukrainian.

By that point, Kirill had moved to Barcelona to work out of the Preply office there (they opened that location in 2018, and by 2021, it had grown to 300 people). They had recently raised a large round of capital and, in order to scale, attract talent, and have a global presence, they needed offices in western Europe. The UK is generally considered too expensive, and Brexit shook things up further, so lots of startups migrated to places like Berlin, Spain, and Portugal.

From afar, Kirill and the Preply team didn't stop until every colleague was relocated, along with many of their families and extended families (even numerous pets!).

In our interview, he described himself on a scale of one to ten as a "nine" for resilience.

"Why do you think that is?" I asked him. "What made you so adaptable and resilient?"

"Stubbornness," he replied with a glint in his eye, adding, "Just refusing to give up."

I sensed that fierceness in Kirill when I'd met him back in 2015 when he was going through the Techstars Berlin program; I was Managing Director of a Techstars program in NYC at the time and had interacted with Kirill's team during the mentor "office hours" we regularly held.

I've always struggled with foreign languages despite having lived around the world, so the concept of Preply appealed to me personally. I had this horribly mean Spanish teacher in middle school who looked like she'd just walked out of an El Greco painting, and that really turned me off to learning Spanish. I also had gone to a French preschool, and the teacher I had there was equally grating, making us eat stinky cheese for snack time and sing "Alouette" ten times a day. Language did not come easy to me, and my teachers really hadn't helped the cause. Preply seemed to be about making learning languages fun and approachable with expert tutors who you can actually relate to. One of their mantras—"At Preply, we are unlocking human potential through learning"—resonated so strongly with me, my life, and how I approached my own business ventures.

Plus, I'm a sucker for scrappy people and teams, and the fact that they were in the room in Berlin showed their mettle. A mentor named Semyon Dukach had suggested Kirill and the Preply team attend Techstars Berlin; they applied and were invited there for final interviews, which is a two-day session where local mentors and investors and other Techstars MDs are invited to help select the new incoming Techstars class.

At the time, though, as Ukraine didn't have a free visa regime, they had to apply for visas to go to Germany, a process that normally took two or three weeks. But the interviews were happening the following week, and Kirill knew they couldn't miss them, because, while they could potentially do them virtually, their chances for admission to the program would be significantly lower. So, Kirill and his co-founder found a way to connect to the German Embassy in Kyiv and plead their case up the ladder. They received their visas a few hours before boarding their flight to Berlin.

I wasn't an investor in Preply, just a super fan. Right before I started writing this book, they raised a whopping $70 million Series C round of funding, which was an unbelievable feat considering the funding pullback happening in tech, especially at the growth stage. Since 2022, venture funding in Europe had dropped by 50 percent, and times were tough for founders trying to raise capital.

That takes us right back to the adaptability that is Kirill's hallmark, which certainly didn't start with the invasion of Ukraine.

He was born there in 1986, a few months after the Chernobyl nuclear disaster. His parents were also scrappy— and competitive overachievers, according to Kirill—especially his mom. Both had a deep influence on him growing up and, of course, today.

The collapse of the Soviet Union in 1991 was the welcome moment of modernization and independence for Ukraine, and the Bigai family was overjoyed by the new world order. When Kirill was eight years old, his dad became an entrepreneur, and Kirill just knew. "I *had* to be an entrepreneur," he told me. From that moment on, he said, "I took that life as a given." But first, he decided to work as an engineer, designer, and product manager for a few different companies in order to make some money and gain experience (though he was soon bored to death).

Simultaneously, he was determined to become a better English speaker and to learn Spanish (serving him well years later when he and his family moved to Barcelona). The problem he ran into was that it was incredibly difficult to find language schools in Ukraine that could accommodate his busy schedule with any sort of flexibility. *How amazing would it be,* he thought, *to have a website where you can find English—or any other—language courses quickly?*

So, Kirill started building his company with that in mind and then quickly pivoted to an adjacent idea: a marketplace for tutoring, which he and his team decided to launch in the US.

This was obviously a huge move into a massive—and very foreign—market and culture.

Semyon, the person that inspired Kirill's application to Techstars Berlin, was not only his mentor but also an early Preply investor who lived in Boston and encouraged the team to take that leap.

Kirill had not yet been to the US, but it was the dream for his company to set up shop there because, he told me, "There's a mythology around the US and the American dream—that if you go to the US, suddenly everything starts happening. So that's what we followed, and we landed in Boston."

Not only was that his first trip to America, it was his first to any English-speaking country at all. He had traveled a bit before then but only as a tourist, never living the day-to-day life of a native. From my own travels, I know how difficult that is.

Kirill laughed as he told me about doing things like going to a restaurant and listening to the server list the specials of the night. "They described the dishes and used fancy words, and I was like, *oh, my gosh, I don't understand a word,*" he said, his eyes crinkling in delight at the memory. For the record, he speaks excellent English now—yet another testament to his adaptability!

Kirill might be a faster learner than most, but it was there in our conversation that he described the need for humility in any learning process, especially ones that are uncomfortable (because aren't they all, at least to some degree?).

"I don't think it's easy to learn if you don't appreciate that you don't know a lot," he shared with me, adding, "And to appreciate that you don't know a lot, you need to be more on the humble side. I think that your learning curve and your humility are very closely connected."

❦❦

Kirill decided he wanted to create a global company even coming from a distant tech ecosystem like Kyiv without any attendant global advantages or privileges, nor ever having traveled that much. He rose to the challenge of conducting high-level business, all in English, when at first, he didn't speak it very well. His company came close to dying on the vine multiple times. He launched three products, the first two failing "horribly" (his word, not mine!). Many people doubted the Preply business model in the early days, and he had to address skepticism at every turn. Fundraising, he said, "was almost never easy" for them. Kirill and his team worked for months and months, sweating over minimal revenue growth, unable to pay themselves.

He made it through a revolution, then the onslaught of a war. Even with that fear, pandemonium, and disruption—his own personal "mission impossible" as he'd called it—there was no negative impact on Preply's growth.

"We like it here in Barcelona. It's a very good city for living," he told me, adding sadly, "Though, I miss Kyiv and Ukraine every day, especially now. Given the growth and trajectory of the business, in the future, I will likely have to spend my time primarily [in Barcelona] or in the US. Living away is complicated and especially painful at the moment. One day, I certainly hope to return to Ukraine."

We hear the lore of the massive success of certain startups out of the gates, but Preply grew by (often tiny) step after step over the course of an entire decade, leapfrogging through and over massive challenges to where it stands right now—a dominant player in the market, with a huge role in language learning on a global scale, well on its way to becoming a billion-dollar company. Kirill's ability to adapt to circumstances—being elastic—that others might find entirely insurmountable was the catalyst for that inspiring build.

KEY INSIGHTS:
KIRILL AS AN ELASTIC FOUNDER

» ***Practice resilience religiously.*** On his life journey, Kirill went through, among other things, the Chernobyl disaster, the Soviet Union's dissolution and transition, and the challenges of building a startup in a remote place like Ukraine. With all of that and more, he continued to consciously pick himself up and move forward from even the toughest experiences. That created in him a "bank" of resilience that allowed him to spring into action to immediately help evacuate and save his team, family, and friends at the start of the current war.

» ***Embrace the unknowns.*** As humans, we find comfort in the known—and it's notoriously difficult to break away from that—but it's *the* way to grow. Kirill as an Elastic knowingly did (and does) this time and again, first by going to Boston and then moving to Barcelona.

» ***Empathy carries opportunity.*** Kirill's empathy has shown up in his life in so many ways, not least with what became his professional *raison d'être*—he was originally interested in learning new languages (like English and Spanish) so he could better understand and connect with other people. That desire ended up offering him the life he is living now as a high-growth founder in that very space.

CHAPTER 6

CHINA

The first time I applied for a visa to China, it was unceremoniously rejected. The form required me to input my employer's details, and I had naively written "BBC" (where I worked at the time).

Apparently, that wasn't going to fly without some further explanation because the BBC, like other Western news outlets, was in a gray zone in terms of their ability to operate openly in China. But the company had a point of contact based in Beijing, and he could fix anything. (I always attributed it to his name being Mathieu, which seemed mysterious and special-agent-esque.) Mathieu instructed me on exactly how to fill out the form and then told me to hand off my passport to a special agency in midtown Manhattan. I cringed at the idea of parting with my beloved passport, but at this point, I was out of options. Then, like magic, a few hours later my visa and passport appeared at my apartment, just in time for my flight.

Since the visa process was less than straightforward, I was wondering how the BBC could even have an office in Beijing, but when I arrived, fresh off a long flight, it all made more sense: the sign on the door read Worldwide Knowledge Business Consulting Company Limited.

"Welcome to China," Mathieu said drolly, noticing me studying the sign with wide eyes.

Western media outlets do, of course, exist in China, but they operate under the radar and are permitted and then quickly shut down depending on the day. It's fascinating because at, for example, upscale hotels in Beijing, a person staying there can typically access media, like CNN and other sources; the government doesn't block it (or they at least allow the VPN). But if you go across town to someone's home, they may not have access. It was a strange little bubble I found myself in.

A few days before the visa fiasco, I'd been asked to go to China to better understand the digital opportunities and challenges there with respect to licensing of content. And although this fell outside of my official role, I'd learned that when the CEO asks you to go, you go. Plus, I was curious and excited for my first visit to China.

But since it was such an unfamiliar place and this would be my first trip there, I was also a tad nervous to be there on my own for a few weeks. So, as I tend to do, I reached out to two of my favorite colleagues—one who ran the digital games group out of LA and one who ran travel strategy in Melbourne—and convinced them to join the expedition.

Armed with the best wingmen, I set out to meet with all the leading digital companies across Beijing and Shanghai (like Youku and Weibo, the Chinese versions of YouTube and Twitter) to forge some licensing deals. Later in the trip, we planned to take the startup temperature in China and meet with founders and VCs.

We'd head into meetings where there were sometimes thirty young employees sitting around a giant table, and though that also included translators, none of us really understood much of what the other was saying! What did come across very clearly, though, was the massive reality check I was facing.

People don't realize this, but outside of their news service, the BBC has the largest archives of any natural history, historical, and documentary content—and that was what we were trying to negotiate in these deals. When we asked each company about their interest in licensing our content, we were met with blank stares. Why would they need to "license" the BBC content when they had access to it already? In other words, our intellectual property did not exactly have strong legal precedent in China.

This sentiment was repeated over and over during my trip, and I was dreading having to tell the CEO that we did not, in fact, *have* a China strategy at all, which was not a message he'd want to hear. I threw my hands up, bought myself some time, and decided to experience the local Beijing flavor instead.

And what better way to understand a city and its people than to hit the nightclubs! My chaperone, Mathieu, had a long list of places that he was excited for us to visit, so he instructed me to find some sequined pants and sparkles and be ready to be picked up at the hotel at 11:00 p.m. Luckily, I'm not a person who needs a ton of sleep.

Naively, I had assumed that gay clubs were an underground thing (at best) in Beijing, but wow, was I wrong.

One funny thing I learned, though (and as the *New York Times* later reported), the word "comrade" (or "*tongzhi*" in Mandarin), which had historically been the term for communist leaders, has been appropriated (and used even more liberally) as slang by LGBTQ+ people in China to refer to each other.

Our first stop was to a multi-story venue called Destination, located in the Sanlitun district in northeast Beijing. It certainly lived up to its name, as it held a traditional nightclub on the ground floor, a VIP lounge on the second floor, and an art gallery, yoga, and dance studio above. The NYC nightlife scene has a lot to learn from the clubs in China, where there seems to be a little something for absolutely everyone.

While I'm always up for a good dance party, when it comes to food, I'm a bit pickier, which I know might seem strange given all of the places I go to and the cuisines that are offered to me. This pickiness came into play on another night, when we were attending a work dinner with a few of the Beijing-based VCs and larger corporate execs we'd started to meet along the way. We headed over to the restaurant, a cavernous place hidden deep inside a nondescript office building, where we were escorted into a private room.

By the time we'd arrived (Beijing traffic is no joke), the Lazy Susan (yes, you read that right—there was a rotating shelf of food for us to choose from) at the center of the large banquet-style table was spinning with an assortment of mystery dishes. As a pescatarian at the time, I tried ever so politely to inquire about the food and whether or not it contained any meat. "Maybe just a little," the waiter replied with a wave of his hand, brushing off my question and concerns.

The alcohol was also flowing, and Mathieu had told me it's rude in China to turn down a drink when offered, so he advised me to take one sip to be polite and then push the glass to the side. The mystery food kept spinning toward me, and the strong drinks kept flowing, and I definitely could not keep up.

Luckily, I was seated next to a large, decorative potted plant with flowing leaves and branches that enveloped my entire side of the table. So, when my glass was refilled yet again, I'd covertly dump it into the base of the plant just to my right. This continued for several hours until the plant was completely soaked and reeking of baijiu, a local spirit often served at large gatherings and paired with a multi-course meal.

I know I've mentioned this before, and while it might be hard to believe given some of my adventures with people around the globe, I'm an introvert, and after several hours of talking and being "on," I need to recharge with some much-needed alone time. But after that dinner, I was still wired from the experience and knew sleep was not going to be possible any time soon.

I said my goodbyes and returned to the Park Hyatt where I was staying and went up to the China Bar, the top floor lounge that I hoped would provide some prime people-watching. I was not disappointed; the scene was right out of a movie like *Lost in Translation*, where lonely Bill Murray-esque types sat by themselves, drowning their sorrows in glasses of whiskey as other well-heeled people filtered in and out.

While the vibe in the lounge eventually started to border on creepy—I'm pretty sure one group of besuited businessmen thought I was an escort by the way they were trying to catch my eye—the views from the sixty-fifth floor extended for miles, and you could see past a couple of the rings of the city (Beijing consists of several concentric circles from the city center out), which was mesmerizing.

It was there that I realized just how big Beijing is, with a population of 22 million and a sprawling geographic footprint. Surely with that many people and seemingly endless tech talent, China would quickly outpace the world in terms of tech and innovation, and I started daydreaming about the opportunities that would continue to grow there.

But even with that, I knew I needed to stop procrastinating the call to the CEO and tell him we had no viable China strategy—the thing that I'd been tasked first and foremost to help figure out. He wasn't super pleased to hear my assessment of the situation but, in truth, he was not surprised. And since I saved him the time and energy of taking the trip himself, he was *mostly* appreciative of my efforts.

卆⽞

China's startup scene dates back to the early 2000s when foreign capital started making its way into the country. Deep-pocketed international groups like Softbank (originating in Japan) and Naspers (originating in South Africa) played an important part in kick-starting the first wave of internet entrepreneurship by investing into the startups that would become some of the most successful and iconic companies in China.

In the last decade, the government and state-backed funds, plus foreign investors, have all supported the rise of the startup ecosystem with cash and a (relatively) friendly regulatory environment that allowed companies like Tencent, Alibaba, Baidu, Didi, WeChat, and Xiaomi to thrive. While the first wave of successful Chinese startups may have taken inspiration from Western companies (Baidu is a search giant similar to Google, and Didi is the dominant ride-sharing app similar to Uber), the second wave of startups building in AI and autonomous vehicles, for example, are China-first models that some Western entrepreneurs are now taking inspiration from.

To truly be global, many successful startups in China have developed their own flavor of company-building, influenced by a mix of MBA programs at US business schools and more traditional Chinese culture. The backgrounds of startup founders there have also evolved from Ivy-League educated Chinese returnees to a broader-based demographic where most anyone with a startup idea can find resources and support.

As an outsider, I see China as a unique market with a specific business culture—those familiar with the "996" working hour system (working 9:00 a.m. to 9:00 p.m. six days a week) may find it intense! But being from New York, I don't really blink at that, and maybe in part from that grinding influence, local startups have leapfrogged ahead in cutting-edge technologies and have built strong foundations for successful global scaling. It's so interesting: China, on one hand, is insular, yet it's also very outward-facing in its innovation.

And that dichotomy—or maybe it's a paradox—extends to politics, too, as China barrels ahead on the startup scene and also on the world stage as a full-fledged superpower. The US government has been making moves to curb investment into Chinese companies (and venture funds like Sequoia Capital have split off their China operations so they proactively get ahead of any regulatory issues they might face). Similarly, there is talk of legislation that would ban TikTok (shaking both the startup and creator worlds to their cores) if its China-based owner doesn't sell its stake, positing that the company is a national security threat in its current form. What all of that ultimately translates to in terms of the business/startup world remains to be seen—but like China itself, it will be far from uninteresting.

Despite all of those regulatory hurdles and political tension, China is only second to the US both in terms of the number of unicorns (300+) and the total amount of funding raised by startups. They are moving at an incredible pace across sectors like artificial intelligence, semiconductors, and e-commerce, which sets up yet another US and China race (of sorts)—but in my opinion, it's one that will be dynamic as well as nail-biting. I left China after a few weeks, light on business accomplishments but rich on culture and new first-hand knowledge of this amazing and fascinating country.

As mentioned earlier, the secondary characteristic of MOXIE centers around extreme self-reliance and forging a path against the odds. Many people develop Moxie as they encounter challenges along the way and learn how to overcome them. Sometimes Moxie is not just about being out-

wardly bold, confident, and opinionated but rather having the ability to face inner fears and unknown outcomes.

MOXIE IN ACTION:

» *Conquer your fears through preparation.* I was rather nervous about going to China, especially as my visa was originally rejected. I was literally sweating going through immigration when they asked me why I was entering the country; I had an actual script to repeat that I'd memorized. Even the most Moxie-filled people I know have insecurities or are scared sometimes, but the difference with them is they bravely move forward, often by being very prepared.

» *Remember to sparkle.* Beijing was not the closed society that I had thought it would be, at least not in the ways that I expected. When I was told to find a club outfit and get ready for a night out, I happily obliged. There are always ways—and reasons—to turn on your inner light.

» *Be bold (and sometimes, fake it till you make it).* The only way I was going to find out if the local tech companies were going to pay for content was if I asked them point-blank. It turns out they were not going to do so, but it took chutzpah to sit in the room with them and ask!

HANHAN XU, CO-FOUNDER OF WATERDROP INSURANCE MARKETPLACE

Though I'd met HanHan through a friend of a friend, right away, she felt like a kindred spirit, and from minute one, our conversation for *Venture Everywhere* was bursting with her reflections (on herself and the world around her), her transparency, her self-awareness and vulnerability, and her tenacity—or, what I like to call in this book, her Moxie.

HanHan's parents were high school teachers, and before that, she told me she came from a long line of peasants. And though her parents had never really traveled, they were very open-minded to literature, philosophy, history, and anything else they could pass along. They taught her to understand both broadly and deeply everything going on in the world and to see things from different (and sometimes competing) perspectives, which offered her a conduit to her later life in the land of startups. Open-mindedness runs deep in HanHan.

One way I really related to HanHan was through her early desire to be an artist. As I wrote in Chapter 1, I've always had a love of art and have exercised my right brain not only through appreciation but through sculpture and painting. (I thought I'd be a fine arts major in college, but things didn't work out that way!) In fact, a lot of founders I know have some sort of artistic side or passion; outside of HanHan (and me), at least two of them show up in this book: Mark Finn (Australia) and Gaby (US). There must be some sort of creative gene underpinning founders in competitive business spaces that allows them to open up to ideas and go with the flow, iterating and riffing along the way, not to mention borrowing from the master that came before, as many artists do.

HanHan pivoted from art and onto a very different route, the "low-risk" one as she called it, achieving entry into the business school at Peking University, which is a feat: it's insanely competitive and usually only the number one and number two in the college admission exam in each province gets in.

"I've always wanted to move away from home, move away from my parents," she told me, adding with a grin, "And have the liberty to be my own woman."

After B-school, all of HanHan's friends were going into investment banking or consulting at top companies, but here is where she realized, as she told me, "There's something different about me compared to my schoolmates." As they embarked on earning great salaries and living very low-risk lives, HanHan started to think differently, and that involved a closer look at the Internet, which she (along with millions of other people) started to see as the baseline for the future, especially in business.

She took a job at a boutique investment bank that specialized in helping entrepreneurs secure funding from institutional investors. Because of the huge gap of information between the two, it was crucial to get them aligned in terms of understanding and interest and to make deals happen so the entrepreneurs could get the money to build their businesses.

"It was rewarding," said HanHan, but after she learned what it took to be a banker, she (you guessed it) got bored.

Of the next two options in front of her—becoming an investor or working on the ground in a growing business—she felt a calling to get into the weeds and help another company build something…and to determine if she had what it took to be a founder in the future.

Before that future came to fruition, though, HanHan took her practice run, helping to build tech company ByteDance (now best known as the owner of controversial social media behemoth TikTok), where she joined as a chief of staff to the founder, giving her a front row seat to what being a founder requires and prepping her for that down the road.

ByteDance grew from twenty-some employees to thousands during her tenure there, and it achieved hyper growth, so she clearly saw and learned a lot. But the voice calling her to entrepreneurship kept getting louder and clearer until she finally enunciated it: "I'm a founder. I want to be a founder, and I want to have a place, a field, that I can practice and be that," she said. "Not in my mind, but actually in real life. I'm ready to get behind the steering wheel and drive, not sit shotgun anymore."

Even with that determination and readiness, though, HanHan became founder in a more roundabout way. Her company Waterdrop Insurance Marketplace had originally been founded by a man, and she joined soon after as co-founder. The vision—trying to build a safety net for ordinary people by innovating insurance—drew her in.

Soon after she joined the company, she felt that the original product (crowd insurance) the company was building was "off." It was hard to understand from a user point of view, and growth became challenging. Soon user growth became stagnant altogether.

HanHan did not give up and eventually came up with the idea to evolve the core business by rolling out a new product: a crowdfunding platform serving families struggling with critical illness and also suffering from financial distress due to huge medical bills. This is a big pool of the population whose problem is overlooked, and the current system is not equipped to help. This was the problem really worth solving and it also showed huge potential for growth.

HanHan led Waterdrop to become the largest crowdfunding platform in the world, growing to 300 million users in three years, while helping millions of families in distress along the way.

🐇🐇

When HanHan mentioned to me that she's (literally) one of the best female heli-skiers (the type of skiing where a person is transported to the top of a massive mountain via helicopter, dropped off, then left to their own devices to whittle their way down) in all of China, my jaw dropped. And she didn't even grow up skiing, because the city where she lived as a child near Shanghai didn't ever see snow.

Her eyes lit up when she described the rush she gets from the sport. "When you're out in the field, *off-piste*, in order to stay on top of the game and get out in one piece, the level of situational awareness needed is intense. There are so many things you need to take in; you breathe and interact with the entire surrounding, not just by your nose, your mouth…you breathe with every cell you have, so you are truly present with all five senses."

"And you stay on top, ride on the edge, and you ride along with the flow that surrounds you," she continued, "and only then you can be at your best; you can truly assess and face risk and adjust yourself to embrace the risk without actually running yourself into too many roadblocks along the way. That is the best feeling. It's a flow state."

We discussed the unbelievable similarities of that type of skiing and being a founder.

"It's so similar: how you actually see the risks, how you perceive them, how you make intellectually honest decisions about them," HanHan said. "And the way you see challenges, the way you face them, the way you embrace them, and the way you conquer them."

And, finally, she concluded, "One extremely important thing is that speed is your friend, but you also need to know how to control your speed. To run a startup, you need to know how to be nimble and, at the same time, be robust."

Speaking to HanHan made me feel like I was getting a master's degree in philosophy—I loved her take on everything, and I wanted to get deeper into how she transitioned into being a founder of a huge startup. Even for a "speed-lover" like her, that takes a lot of courage. Where did that come from, I wondered?

"First it's the calling," she said, "the calling to become who I am. Deep down, I know that I'm a doer and a builder, and I've known that for a while."

Next, it was simply her winding path to take. "I'm always good with puzzles, to get grounded in the present, and feel through the puzzles as I go."

HanHan stayed at Waterdrop for four years, taking the company through their best and worst times, through fierce competition, through regulatory hurdles, and through a series of PR crises. At one point, an undercover report found staff signing up patients to fill quotas, exaggerating their stories and failing to check financial details, causing a major controversy and major problems for Waterdrop. But even with that, the company was huge, and the wins outshone the losses. But HanHan's time at Waterdrop was done.

I could feel the bittersweet tinge the conversation took as we discussed HanHan's departure from Waterdrop, and I asked her about the fact that, these days, her name is seldom mentioned as a co-founder of the company. All discourse and media around it focuses on the original male founder, and her name isn't anywhere on the record. "Thanks for noticing that," she said sadly. "It's a common thing that women face, right? We don't get enough credit." It was at this point in our discussion that HanHan (and by extension me) choked up, and her eyes filled with tears.

"The things we do, the things we try—they're not going to get recognized quickly." She continued after a beat. "Sometimes it forces you to give up the things that you created. It's definitely tough."

A few minutes later, I could see her resilience in action as HanHan rallied, perking up to tell me more forcefully, "And just because the recognition doesn't come soon enough, that's not a reason for us to give up the fight. If we don't keep up with it, the world is going to lose even more."

I can sense that the open-mindedness HanHan learned from her parents and that followed her all through her life gives her the wherewithal to keep putting one foot in front of the other and to continue to see things as opportunities, where other people would see stop signs.

"Plus," she laughed, "I'm petite. Even low-hanging fruit could be a challenge for me. So, I don't go looking for low hanging fruit."

After laughing (and crying) with HanHan over our long conversation, I left it feeling like I'd learned a new definition and embodiment for her type of Moxie—and certainly a new definition of success—built entirely on an open-minded mentality, always ready to embrace a new reality.

KEY INSIGHTS:
HANHAN AS A FOUNDER OF MOXIE

» *Self-acceptance is key.* People make mistakes and misjudgments (and regularly—you can't be human and avoid that!), and lots of things go wrong in life, but moving forward and being successful revolve around both self-awareness and self-acceptance, not to mention self-forgiveness. It's a reminder that things will be what they will be, and it's better to reach your flow state than dwell on the "what-ifs."

» *Engage in radical transparency (where appropriate).* HanHan was an open book, willing to share her story (both the ups and downs) so she can continue to learn and grow. This vulnerability is important in that it empowers other people to do the same.

» *Impact over ego.* She received no real credit for co-founding a wildly successful company, but she's not looking back or getting hung up on that. The most important thing for HanHan was going on a journey for herself that, in some way, made the world a better place.

CHAPTER 7

EGYPT

Growing up in New York City, one of my favorite activities was going to the Egyptian Wing at the Metropolitan Museum of Art.

I'd sit enraptured for hours after school, drawing the Temple of Dendur and other fascinating antiquities. I even made a model of the temple using sugar cubes for a class project in fifth grade. Thus began my fixation on the country of Egypt, and when I finally got the chance to visit the real place, all my (sweetest!) dreams came true.

Around 2018, I was faced with a dilemma. Massive amounts of capital had flooded into the early-stage venture arena in the US, and that meant everyone and their mother started investing in startups. Part of this was fueled by a long stretch of low interest rates where investors were looking for higher returns and money seemed to be free. What this meant for investors like me is that startup valuations increased significantly, and the value proposition of an accelerator like the one I ran diminished.

It became harder and harder for me to source great companies based in NYC that would join my accelerator program (because of the economics associated with the investment), so I had to forge a plan. My best idea was to increase the surface area of where I recruited companies from, and that led me to focus on startups in underserved tech ecosystems where the opportunity to join a top accelerator program was still very appealing—which is why I found myself in Cairo, meeting with tech founders.

Cairo is a place of contrasts, where ancient monuments exist alongside modern skyscrapers and frenetic markets. This juxtaposition of modernity and tradition contributes to a unique atmosphere that was compelling to a city person like me. There is just *so much* to see: the streets are bustling with people selling things pop-up style, with markets and street vendors at every turn. I was struck by the mix of old and new, with some locals openly practicing customs deeply rooted in their cultural heritage. Many people (men and women) wear a *galabeya* (a long-sleeve cotton tunic) and a *keffiyeh* (headscarf) while others could've been plucked from the streets of Fifth Avenue in New York.

The Egyptians we encountered were incredibly friendly and welcoming and quick to offer us hibiscus (*karkadeh*) or mint tea. As an American woman, I did find the male gaze and attitude to be a bit intense, but it was nothing I couldn't handle. In fact, several people thought I looked Egyptian—a huge compliment!

I'm somewhat reluctant to admit this, because I usually pride myself on being an anti-tourist, or at least more of a local in most places I go, but I've always wanted to see the Sound and Light show at the pyramids of Giza (located on the outskirts of Cairo) after dark. While it's true that you can see them lit up while walking the streets of Giza, I was set on the whole light show experience.

The area around the pyramids is what you would expect from a global destination: lively, packed with wide-eyed tourists and a souvenir salesman for each one. Walking through, you get really good at saying, "No thank you...no thanks... thanks, but no!"

The light show is an hour long and narrated with the history and archaeological details of the pyramids, complete with music and brightly colored laser projections. The night we went, we missed the English language show and ended up with a jolly group of sunburned Germans watching it in their native tongue. It was so much fun and a big step out of everyone's language comfort zone. The following night, we had dinner at the Mena House Hotel, and I was able to appreciate all the more the stunning pyramid views after having had the opportunity to see them front and center in all their lit-up glory.

On another evening, I also had the opportunity to attend an open kitchen restaurant (think part cooking class, part being in a chef's kitchen), which was a highlight of my Cairo trip. If you're into carb loading, you'll love the national dish of *koshari*—a mix of rice, lentils, pasta, chickpeas, and onions, topped with a spicy tomato sauce. Many Egyptians also have a sweet tooth, so to my delight (remember, I started my Egyptian journey when I was a kid with sugar cubes), we topped off meals with a variety of phyllo dough-wrapped pastries.

I was, of course, especially interested to learn more about the origins of the local startup scene in Egypt, considering that the Arab Spring in 2010—which helped bring political and social changes with an increased focus on entrepreneurship as a means of economic development—went down at the same time I was running my own startup.

Many of us watched it closely, hopeful that more stable times would come to the country and that even more entrepreneurial opportunities would materialize. We were not disappointed.

Over the next decade, the government, along with various incubators and accelerators, started heavily supporting startups through programs providing mentorship, community, and capital. As with many growing tech ecosystems in developing countries, fintech won the hearts and minds of the community, first with startups addressing financial inclusion, payment solutions, and digital banking. Companies like Fawry and Paymob made significant strides, attracting both regional and global investors, and a newly formed, government-backed fund—Egypt Ventures—was created.

500 Global (one of the most well-known accelerators in the world) has a collaboration with the Information Technology Industry Development Agency (ITIDA) in Egypt, providing local startups and innovators with global opportunities through their programs, curated events, and strategic partnerships. It's always fun for me to come across the 500 Global programs and communities because the founder was the very first investor to my second startup back when the firm was a small operation in Mountain View, California.

Because of that growing cultural belief in innovation, Egypt has a vibrant stable of local founders, many who have worked at startups around the region (some even in the US) and has a shot at outpacing other countries with startups focused on healthcare, agriculture, and climate, in addition to fintech and payments.

The infrastructure for the burgeoning startup community is starting to catch up, with new spaces like Consoleya starting to pop up. Consoleya, a co-working space in an old part of downtown Cairo (an area that's home to a growing number of tech startups) is the brainchild of a woman named Hanan Abdel Meguid and her business partners. It's a unique and modern space in an almost ancient Egyptian setting, with a mix of government groups, corporates, and startups all sharing desk space under one roof.

Consoleya is also the home of Plug and Play, the Egyptian division of the well-known tech center in Silicon Valley (if you've been to SV, you've likely driven by their large office building just off the 101), which is a platform to connect startups to industry; it works as a bridge between Silicon Valley and dozens of locations around the world as one of the largest innovation-enablement platforms worldwide.

[Side note: I shared the stage with Saeed Amidi, the founder of Plug and Play at the LEAP conference in Saudi Arabia, whom I'll talk about in Chapter 12; he and I dug into the topic of "Investing in the Future of Humanity." We share the thesis that innovation is everywhere, and we should be investing where the best founders are, wherever they are. We also talked about what it's like to open up a new market and being the connective tissue between the local founders and the US market.]

During my visit to Cairo, I was also intrigued to hear about a program called WomanUp Weeknights, which took place at the storied GrEEK Campus, a renowned innovation hub in the city.

I decided to crash it. At the event, I was thrilled to find a mix of women founders and tech workers from a variety of backgrounds who all shared a vision for a more inclusive tech community in Egypt.

They gathered around me, asking a lot of questions about my experiences in tech. It was eye-opening to hear them relate how they were overcoming cultural and societal challenges to do the work they loved. I found out later that it was one of several campus events supporting and empowering women in tech.

I walked away from that night and that trip feeling like progress—in all of its forms, even in places like Egypt where it's not intuitive or always visible—is an inevitable part of any well-organized system.

The second appearance of SYSTEMATIC as one of the characteristics comprising the Everywhere Mindset is intriguing because it showcases one of the places in the

world that feels the least systematic on the surface (Cairo and the chaotic nature of the city). But going one layer deeper, navigating a place like Cairo requires a more holistic understanding of how the neighborhoods came about and were structured from a historical perspective—it makes much more sense to a local. Clearly, this is less familiar to people in the US since the country and its cities are so young by comparison. That shows two things: though some people might be (or become) Systematic in response to their environment, it also shows that the founder persona is highly mutable.

SYSTEMATIC IN ACTION:

» **Build on what you love.** Whether it's me with my tiny sugar cube Egyptian temple models or someone building a massive tech company infrastructure, it's important to follow the road to what lights you up, because Systematic does not mean a lack of passion— in fact, often it's quite the opposite.

» **Find patterns with process.** The parts and their result (the whole), are important, of course: when we think about something like the pyramids, each stone block in and of itself was massive, and together they created one of the wonders of the natural world. It's almost mind-boggling to imagine how that was done, but even if the details are still a mystery to scientists, I do know one thing, which is that each small cog in that creation had its own process, ultimately contributing to the greater good.

» **Share the system.** In Egypt, women are making strides in tech and across the country more generally. They may still have a way to go (as do women in most places, quite frankly), but this early opening is a great demonstration of the successes that broader mind-share in a system can produce.

JACQUES MARCO, FOUNDER OF AXIS

The first time I met Jacques Marco, the Egyptian founder of the payment platform company Axis Pay, we chatted and bantered and exchanged ideas for so long that I was over thirty minutes late to my next meeting—and if you've guessed anything at all about me at this point, it's that I'm *always* on time.

My business partner Scott had known Jacques for some time and urged me to meet him when he was visiting New York, but I was reluctant. I am, of course, always happy to meet a fantastic founder, but the prospect of carving our way into Egypt gave me pause. Investing there, like in many emerging markets, can be tough—not only is there the usual existential startup risk of investing into early-stage companies before they've established product/market fit, but there's added risk relating to currency instability and potential political turmoil.

But after our breakfast, I immediately called Scott, and when he answered, I told him without preamble, "We need to be involved in anything Jacques is working on."

Jacques was born and raised in Alexandria, and at fifteen years old, he decided to leave Egypt to go to boarding school in the UK to focus on learning English. He was very clear about taking this path in order to "grow out of his shell," as he described it to me, and even though he was a very shy kid, he got to make friends from places like Italy, Germany, Britain, and more, which irreparably cracked that shell.

"I never looked back," he said. "I was on my way."

Though the choice to go to boarding school might have added an extra layer on the foundation to what blossomed into his Everywhere Mindset, Jacques's entrepreneurial roots had taken hold when he was much younger, and in the same way mine did: in his grandparents' home!

Jacques's grandmother was a lawyer and had her own law firm (this really impressed me, of course; strong women always do), and his grandfather would have Bloomberg News on the TV at all hours. From about the age of five, Jacques would sit with him, glued to the market like most kids watched *The Lion King*, fascinated by the tickers showing the stocks going up and down, enthralled by the idea of becoming an expert in what was happening on the screen.

Naturally, this fascination with Wall Street led him to enroll at New York University, thinking banking was the eventual route for him. During his time there, Jacques applied for internships at all the big banks.

And was rejected by all of them.

His first pivot (a warm-up for any good entrepreneur) was teaching, and he joined the NYU learning center, even creating his own course there. Thinking academia was now the path, he began a master's degree at Columbia University.

And after three months, he left that too.

"It was a waste of money and a waste of time," he told me. "I was escaping life and reality, staying in something that felt easy and comfortable, but what was really next for me?"

Ten years prior, he hadn't ever wanted to return to Egypt, but Jacques did just that to work in—full circle—investment banking. He very quickly grew bored. Incidentally, (outside of, of course, a great idea), boredom is a common reason why founders start companies (myself included—it was one of the reasons I began seeing problems to solve and started my first company to go about solving them).

While Jacques was at NYU, he had used Venmo and thought the peer-to-peer money movement was an innovative concept. Egypt had nothing similar, so things clicked. He took inspiration from a business model that was working in the US, and at the age of twenty-five, along with his brother Karl, he decided to start his first company. This was not a typical startup but a joint venture with a large, established bank in Egypt where the brothers owned a smaller portion of the equity and learned a few lessons about governance, incentives, and the capitalization table along the way.

In the end, the bigger bank bought them out, and they parted ways. Now fresh with all the learnings, Jacques decided to found Axis, a true startup without the wonky structure that the previous company had.

Egypt was still behind other developing tech ecosystems, and entrepreneurship wasn't something people, in general, looked favorably upon in that society. And forget available venture funding—it just didn't exist—so for Jacques, the risk, not to mention the uphill climb, was that much steeper.

But Jacques told me, "I wasn't scared of doing it. I said, *What's the worst-case scenario?* And that's a mechanism I use to think things through: any decision I'm making, I ask that question: *What's the worst that can happen?* And if I'm okay with the worst-case scenario, I'm okay with making the decision."

He went on to say, "If it didn't work out, I would have learned a ton. And then, well, what's the worst thing? I'll just get into one of these MBA programs because I'll have a story that's different from all of the consultants and investment bankers. And then I'll start again."

From the second I met him, Jacques has seemed wise beyond his years; that showed up in his attitude around company building and came across even more when we dove deeper into his comfort with the big decisions he's had to make every step of the way. That became obvious to me as rooted in an adjacent quality—his self-acceptance—something so many people (both in and outside of business) struggle with, but would benefit from.

"It took me a year or two to come to the conclusion that, ultimately, I will not change who I am," Jacques said. "I have my strengths, and I have my flaws. I can work on my flaws a little bit, but at the end of the day, I need to be comfortable making the decisions I'm making. I'll make mistakes. As long as I don't repeat the same mistake twice, I'm fine. You learn by doing, and at every stage of it, you just learn a new part."

But, he admitted, even with that approach, building a company was still a "total black box" that he knew absolutely nothing about, and in the young Egyptian ecosystem, there weren't many resources around to illuminate things.

"People build companies and just figure it out," Jacques said with a shrug.

So, he moved forward into growth mode with Axis Pay, and even though Jacques is a self-proclaimed shy introvert, the right people—whom, he said, "work with you and stay and figure stuff out even when things are not going so well"—were at the center of the momentum.

As was learning how to navigate those relationships.

"You want to have a friendship with your colleagues," he told me, "but at the end of the day, it's still a professional relationship, and in any professional relationship, it can work really well, and it can stop working. And how do you balance this? Friendship is different from work, and I try to keep them separate, and that's why Karl and I are not building another company together, because for us, what's more important is that we're brothers."

I've seen a lot of founders struggle with that tension; you're in the trenches with your team and often experience massive highs and lows, which brings you really close, but you still need to, as Jacques put it, place a "maximum on how close those relationships can get."

He continued, describing a conundrum most founders face at some point or another: "Yes, there are people I'm working with that I really like working with. But at the end of the day, it's still a professional relationship, and I appreciate them. And a big part of why I appreciate them is because they're doing what they need to do. The minute they're not doing what they need to do, it becomes difficult to appreciate them. You can empathize with why they're not doing what they need to do, but what are you going to do? It's not like a friend who's going through a rough patch, and you say, 'All right, I'm here for you, and if I can help, I help. If I can get you through it, I'll get you through it.'"

Unlike in corporate America, which sets up guard-rails for extenuating circumstances, in a startup, those lines become murkier when it's all-hands-on-deck, and a "separation of church and state" of sorts is required in relationships. Setting boundaries is an important skill, and Jacques grasped that early on.

🐦🐦

At a few points during our conversation around the building of Axis Pay, Jacques and I talked about the importance of forcing yourself out of the familiar or easy confines of habit and into something harder, all in order to grow.

Jacques related how, during his early days at NYU, he never raised his hand and asked a question, or really spoke in class at all (a fact that surprised me given his self-assuredness during our conversation for *Venture Everywhere*). But as his time there went on, he forced himself to teach groups and classes, which he said was the scariest (yet ultimately fruitful) thing he could do.

"Going into the class, I'm scared, I'm sweaty, a disaster," he laughed. "But once I'm there, I do it. So, it was just about getting myself into these moments. And the more you do it, the more you feel comfortable with it."

I related to that so much, because I had a very similar experience. I'd always hated public speaking, so when I went to law school, I made myself join moot court, where I found myself arguing on a stage in front of hundreds of other people. It completely ejected me from my own comfort zone, which has served me very well in everything that has since come along in my professional life.

At its core, Jacques's story has a theme of the early part of life and business being the time to learn and then using that knowledge to really grow into the next, even more powerful phase of life and business. Once Axis was established, it started going strong, then started to weather some bumps along the way, like the currency instability in Egypt and the fallout from the 2021 tech bubble.

Jacques always went back to the idea he held firm: "It's the people you have around you across the whole stack, from your partners, investors, shareholders, to the team you build," he said. "That's what makes or breaks a startup." He continued, "So, try to get the right people around you, and get the wrong people out as soon as possible, which is something I didn't do before. The biggest learning is [coming to an] understanding of what I can and can't do."

I think Jacques's clear advantage here is his Everywhere Mindset—living in different places like he did from a super young age, through which, he said, "Your horizon expands."

"But," he added with a rueful note in his voice, "some of it translates, some of it doesn't translate…. I thought building in Egypt would be easier than building elsewhere. It's actually harder," he continued, noting the barriers to company-building in Egypt—such as access to capital, talent with startup experience, and a stable currency—which is only recently starting to change.

He might say that with a bit of resignation, but in the same way he seems to fundamentally accept himself and his decisions, he accepts that paradigm too.

Throughout our talk, I marveled at Jacques's wisdom (which can be very much a part of the Systematic profile)— even at (still) such a young age—and from my vantage point, he's innately a great leader, underscored by his sophisticated communication skills. And since he has such a focus on growing his strengths, I wanted to dig into understanding how he cultivated those capabilities.

At one point, he told me there were some seemingly intractable issues Axis Pay faced, so Jacques organized an internal town hall. He got everyone on the team together, and without a solution in mind, outlined the six challenges they, as a company, were up against. He asked everyone to come up with a contribution to the solutions, then gather in teams to pressure-test those ideas. Finally, they'd straw-man different ideas and make data-driven decisions on what to implement.

But the important thing to him was having everyone partake in the process. "It's all about alignment and level of ownership," he told me.

The town hall idea, he said, is something that's still a work in progress. If he can get the team to work independently without feeling the need to always revert to him, or, if they have a disagreement, to use him as the tiebreaker, that, he said, is effective. It's also a highly systematic way of including his entire team in company growth.

But what I really love about it is that it works in an active, 360-degree way: he has a growth mindset and steps out of his comfort zone, which also means being willing to accept feedback on his own actions and abilities within the company. As such, he blocks time every quarter when he "forces" (his words!) his team to reflect on what went well and what didn't go so well, and he does the same.

Running a company in a place like Egypt can be hectic with political uncertainty, currency issues, and a lack of funding and talent, and as a result, founders like Jacques feel compelled to include a lot more structure and process in their companies (like his hiring process, town halls, and other elements of his leadership and communication)—and they thrive all the more because of this.

KEY INSIGHTS:
JACQUES AS A SYSTEMATIC FOUNDER

» *Start with clarity whenever possible.* Jacques was very sure of his path from a young age, which included going to boarding school in the UK (and learning English). This was the core of his trajectory to becoming a successful founder, and for him, it was non-negotiable out of the gates.

» *Teach to refine.* Though it made him very uncomfortable, Jacques forced himself to become a teacher and tutor (and thus, speak in front of large groups) during his time at NYU. This was a direct line to him becoming the highly sophisticated communicator and consensus-builder he is today.

» *Think global, act local.* Vital for Jacques was seeing the big picture of the world and putting the foundation in place to be able to come back to Egypt to build. This also showed up when he and his brother decided after their first company that it was better to be brothers than business partners—a very mature and big-picture way of thinking—so they went their separate ways in business. [Fun fact: I am an investor in both brothers' startups. Sometimes things work out for a reason!]

CHAPTER 8

THE PHILIPPINES

As I mentioned in the introduction, I was inspired to start my first company after talking to a friend who'd just gotten back from a trip to the Philippines and described the digital/mobile banking that was happening in that country, a far cry from anything I'd heard of at the time. I can't emphasize enough how important this conversation was for my entire professional and personal path, not to mention my forthcoming deep commitment to the startup world.

So, the Philippines, while more distant to me and my life in some ways, is also a pivotal part of this narrative. And while I haven't yet been to Manila to experience the vibrant startup scene there in person, a trip is in the works now that Everywhere Ventures has two investments there.

I have, however, been scuba diving in the Philippine Islands (they have 7,000+ to choose from!) by way of Honduras. Yes, I know, roundabout—but that's how things unfolded....

I went to Honduras to learn how to dive, and my instructor took a shine to me. We ended up hanging out for the duration of my trip. He lived and grew up in Roatan, an island in Honduras, and his mother was from the Philippines, and although he had visited her family a couple of times, he was stunned by the incredible ocean life there.

"If you ever go to Asia," he told me, "find your way to Moalboal and look up my uncle, who will take you to see the sardines."

Ever since he said that, I'd felt the drumbeat of a calling to go to the islands despite the loose connection on the ground and the big hassle to get there. So, more than a decade later, on a work trip to Asia, I found myself booking a flight to Cebu, taking a three-hour shuttle to Moalboal, and tracking down my Honduran dive instructor's now-retired *tiyo* (uncle) to ask him to take me swimming with the sardines.

The first time I saw said sardines (there are around seven million that reside in the waters there), I was snorkeling and freediving, and all at once, they seemed to envelop me in a fish whirlpool. It's freaky to be outnumbered by so many fish but also incredible to be able to swim through them seemingly unnoticed.

Soon it was time to pull the trigger on a proper scuba dive, which I had been procrastinating on doing even though it was really the whole point of my trip. I'd had a bad scuba experience two years earlier and ended up in a decompression cabin, so I certainly had some residual fears, but the calling was too strong. I'd heard so much about the islands and the amazing reef that I braved it and got back in the water.

I was properly blown away. Immediately, I saw, in close proximity, schools of barracuda darting here and there, small reef sharks circling lazily, turtles paddling around, and caves heaving with sea fan coral.

On my final day, I ended up going to Oslob to swim with whale sharks, which are, for reference, as big as NYC buses. Also, I have an (irrational?) fear of sharks, stemming from seeing *Jaws* at an inappropriately young age, and since then, I am never without wide-open eyes scanning the horizon for that telltale fin the minute I enter a body of water.

Once on the boat, I dragged my feet and almost didn't drop into the water, but I ultimately decided it was an excellent way to face that fear and see what I was made of.

It was absolutely surreal getting close enough to touch these beasts. The whole experience was next-level, and once I conquered my fear, I felt like I was walking on air.

I stayed at the Magic Island Dive Resort, which is a quirky place with communal meals and a few private bungalows. It was there, while talking to the dive boat crew and (of course) asking them why Filipinos are often regarded as entrepreneurial, that I first heard the word "*negosyante*," which is Tagalog for "entrepreneur."

They seemed to think that economic reality, coupled with family and community values, were the driving force. Many Filipino entrepreneurs are motivated by a desire to provide for their families and contribute to the well-being of their communities, and this sense of responsibility and interconnectedness fuels their drive to succeed. In fact, my Honduran friend's *tiyo* was a great example: he'd started a dive school in order to make sure his sisters and brothers received good educations and to provide a better life for his children. This was something he couldn't see happening while employed as a fisherman or similar job.

That got me thinking about how, in the Philippines, in both business and life, culture and conviction go hand in hand (and that *really* shines through in this chapter's profile of Great Deals founder Steve Sy) and deeply influence the startup community there.

Up-and-coming countries in Asia, especially the Philippines, are interesting from a tech perspective. With a population of 110 million (the second largest in the region after Indonesia) and a median age of twenty-five, it's a huge—and young—market of tech-savvy citizens who are open to new experiences, creating an atmosphere that's ripe for startup innovation.

Many pundits opine that we're entering the golden era of startups in the Philippines, since the country ranks sixth among startup ecosystems in Southeast Asia and is in fifty-ninth position globally. From 2020 to 2021, venture funding in the country soared from $180 million to $863 million USD.

Areas of development include fintech (as I've mentioned, mobile money offerings date back to the early 2000s in the country, which is early indeed!), Web3 and cryptocurrency, e-commerce, "social commerce," and live-streaming companies. The Philippines has given birth to several standout startups, including two unicorns: Mynt, developer of the mobile wallet Cash, and Voyager Innovations, which is behind the payments platform Maya. The digital economy is very new in the Philippines—the country was mainly analog just a decade ago, and the growth in demand for these new digital goods and services isn't slowing down any time soon.

There are a lot of reasons for the Filipino startup boom, including tax incentives. To boost an entrepreneurial spirit and encourage foreign investment, the Filipino government exempts startups from taxes for the first two years of operations. Also, the economy runs on private consumer spending rather than government capital injections, and the government isn't responsible for a lot of the spending domestically, in contrast to many Western countries. That means Filipinos are used to spending and being consumers, which in turn, provides an attractive market for startups offering new products (physical or digital) combined with easier ways to pay. The growth of the Filipino middle class vindicates that particular market opportunity.

My business partner, Scott, spent a lot of time in the Philippines when he lived in Asia, and we knew we wanted to have a presence there when we started Everywhere Ventures, so we started developing relationships with founders and operators on the ground, some of whom became investors (limited partners) in our fund, and as I mentioned earlier, we partnered with a few as well.

One such company is Podmachine, a podcasting platform whose team is helping Scott and me build out our global podcasting network. The founder, Ron, is one of the hardest-working CEOs I've ever seen; our chats often occur at 11:00 p.m. his time, yet he never sounds anything less than supercharged.

Another of our portfolio founders is Ben Wintle, the founder and CEO of Booky, the leading subscription-based food and lifestyle app designed to discover and make reservations at restaurants, gyms, salons, and spas. Ben is Filipino-British, grew up in Hong Kong, and runs Booky out of Manila. He is a great example of being among a first wave of startup founders in an emerging market, which are often diasporas returning from abroad.

In a few Asian countries, these founders are referred to as "sea turtles," and they bring a network, knowledge, and experience that is essential to building out the ecosystem's foundations and best practices.

And now we're starting to see second-generation Filipino startup founders, born and bred in the Philippines, who bring a different skill set to the table, most prominently their deep, intricate understanding of the local problems they're trying to solve.

Ultimately, though, for educated Filipinos, there's still a hard choice between the traditional corporate route and the startup journey. For many, money hasn't been easy to come by, and the promise of a stable, high-paying job at a multinational continues to be alluring.

Culture also plays a role: Filipino society is conservative, and risk-taking isn't necessarily seen as a virtue. Social stigma about the entrepreneurial/startup path is still a reality, and the tide of conviction in that specific realm is still turning.

Developing CONVICTION is an important tenet of the Everywhere Mindset. Conviction can quietly build as data and new information is gathered, or it can be all at once like an inner force. People who have strong conviction are vocal about it and are also brave insomuch as they have to defend their firmly held beliefs. Conviction can stem from deep inner faith, either in a religious sense or just an inner calling than some people have. In my case, facing fears was not work- or startup-related but rather ocean-related, when I had to slowly build a conviction that getting back in the water after a scuba incident was the right thing to do.

CONVICTION IN ACTION:

> » *Pay attention to the calling.* The calling I felt toward the Philippines showed me the importance of tapping into instincts and intuition. Sometimes things happen and we don't know why, but it's leading us somewhere important—the work of the invisible hand of the metaphysical world, perhaps. That country, (though difficult to get to in more ways than one), was the inspiration for my very first startup, is part of our Everywhere Ventures thesis, and is where our podcast is produced. You may not know the significance of something until later, but pay attention to the deep "knowing" now.

> » *Swim with the sharks.* I'd never recommend jumping into deep water blindly or unsafely, but it was time to

face my dual fear (scuba diving and sharks)—and my conviction about my own growth as a person played a part in doing something I didn't, at first glance, want to do.

» **Consider culture and community.** So much of what we believe is rooted in where we come from. And, as I saw with Filipino entrepreneurs, who wanted to make money to better their lives but also have a micro-level impact in their community, anyone can find inspiration in where they originate.

STEVE SY, FOUNDER OF GREAT DEALS

Though Steve Sy, the Filipino founder of the e-commerce platform Great Deals, is a classic entrepreneur in the truest sense—he told me during our conversation that he's never been "employed" in the corporate world, but instead has been a founder his entire adult life—he doesn't actually come across as what people might envision as an entrepreneur in the startup world. Instead of a recent college grad, at forty-nine years old, he's seasoned, wearing a nice button down (no hoodies on this Zoom call), and working out of a more traditional office setting (probably no beer in the breakroom).

I hadn't known Steve before we sat down for our *Venture Everywhere* conversation, but the people who produce my podcast (the Podmachine team I mentioned earlier) are very sharp and entrepreneurial, always coming up with new products and services relating to podcasting. Since they're also the editors of mine, they always ask me what we look for in founders (and podcast guests).

One day, I asked the founder, Ron, about the startup scene in the Philippines, and he got really excited, telling me, "We're behind the US but catching up quickly and expect to have many more newly minted unicorns in the next few years!"

I told Ron that we sometimes refer to these growth-stage startups as "soonicorns"—and it turned out he had an amazing founder of one that I should meet: Steve Sy.

Right away, I noticed that Steve is really warm, but he also had a gravitas I appreciated. Over the course of our conversation, I learned that fed right into his deep, deep conviction—for entrepreneurship and his company, but also beyond that to his family, and community—all of which was rooted in his religious faith.

〈〉〈〉

Steve was born into family of entrepreneurs (textiles, among other ventures), and he also carried that gene, seeing from a very young age even seemingly small opportunities to create businesses and make money. At eight years old, he sold stickers to his classmates at "retail" prices after buying a whole pad of them and cutting them into individual pieces, earning himself a couple of extra pesos for each in the process.

"We'd been raised to be entrepreneurs in some ways, but nobody actually taught me," he told me. "It was more of an innate thing that I saw and felt the opportunity."

That was a harbinger of the ambition—and audacity—to come for Steve. He started side-hustling in earnest in college (selling watches and T-shirts), all in service of his first business goal, which was earning his first million pesos.

He did that by age twenty.

Shortly thereafter, he got married and was earning a lot of money during that time. "But because of greed," he said solemnly, "I invested my money into scammish ventures and lost and was in debt for thirty-two million pesos or more."

That equates to about $600,000. Steve was all of twenty-seven years old, and it took him another twelve years to pay it off.

"The first year," he told me, "I was still gung-ho, saying to myself, *I'll be able to pay my debt*. But after three, four, five years, you've seen your friends getting cars, buying homes, and you're still paying off your debt. You get depressed; you get discouraged. But the beauty of it is, I persevered because I have my faith."

And that faith not only got him to a debt-free place but into the e-commerce space where he started Great Deals, which he calls his own personal "Promised Land."

He started by selling cell phone accessories during the infancy stage of e-commerce in the Philippines on deal sites like Groupon and Sogo and then on Lazada, which was the Amazon of the Philippines at that time. His light-bulb moment came when he sold out of a few thousand power banks in one day and realized that e-commerce is, as he described it, an "animal." He began studying and learning the business inside and out.

I've seen and worked with all sorts of founders, and Steve falls squarely into what I refer to as the "MBA founder": he saw a white space, worked out the unit economics, and then executed meticulously on his business plan; it's a more clinical view of entrepreneurship. Another example of this is the company Warby Parker, which came together when five students getting MBAs at Wharton identified a market gap in eyewear and found a new way to serve customers.

Driven by his conviction, Steve initially began to grow his business through bootstrapping as a sole proprietor and then switched course in 2020 by raising outside capital in a Series A transaction. Cash was the rocket fuel that Great Deals needed to keep up with demand, and a year later, Steve raised $30 million in a Series B round led by the logistics company Fast Group, whose strategic investment could help them reduce shipping costs.

In 2022, Great Deals was recognized by *Financial Times* as the fastest growing company in Asia Pacific, beating the likes of startups in countries India, Japan, South Korea, Australia, Thailand, and Indonesia.

That was a tremendous amount of growth in a relatively short period of time, and I asked Steve how he learned about leadership and what his path to evolving into a good leader was like, and how that changed as the company scaled.

"I've been active in church groups staffed by volunteers for a long time. And if you've been involved in any type of volunteer group, you know that you need to build consensus to move projects forward," he told me. "I think one of the best ways to learn leadership is to be able to lead volunteers, because if you're leading people you're paying, it's much easier than working with volunteers."

But more important, Steve said, was being the embodiment of the company's core values.

"I provide the vision and mission for our company, which is to uplift Filipino lives through the digital economy," he said. "I present very strong core values: *tapat*, which is integrity; *malasakit* means ownership; and *galing* means excellence in action. So simple that they can be easily communicated across the organization."

Steve went on to tell me he fundamentally believes that their company mission has propelled them to work harder because there's a bigger picture that they all subscribe to—zeroing in on both profitability *and* sustainability.

Part and parcel of that is also what he described as the Four Ps: Profitability, vital to attain its Purpose, which is the second P. Then comes "blessing" your People, and finally, helping your Planet.

I loved hearing that. Steve struck me as very internally aligned, but as with any founder, he'd experienced really tough times, like he shared earlier in our conversation about his major debt.

Another one of those tough times came early in the company's history, when he was being courted by a couple of major health and beauty brands for admission to the Great Deals platform. The problem was, he needed working capital to the tune of 40 million pesos, around $800,000, to be able to get their business.

It was a crossroads for Steve. He told me he asked himself, *Am I going to be just content with the business that I have, or do I take on more business?*

He worried that he might be too greedy and lack the resources for proper expansion, an obvious throwback to the fear he had when he racked up his debt.

So he prayed.

"God said, *I give you this talent, now go and multiply. Go and make use of the talent that I have given you,*" Steve told me. His faith was clearly his anchor.

Now at peace with his chosen path, Steve went about solving the $800,000 (or lack thereof) problem, and that's when investors and funding came in, sending Great Deals to the next (and the next) level, all while his eye never wavered from the bigger vision.

"It's important, vital, to continue to make an impact," Steve said, "because I know Great Deals is not just about me, but also breaking the glass ceiling for a Filipino company to become a global company. Those are the things that make me motivated in terms of overcoming all the challenges that we have faced."

And like many of the people and founders I find myself surrounded by, Steve values the support of the people around him to help him get through it all too. "This is why we pay it forward," he told me earnestly, "because somewhere in our life there are people that have given their life to you, for you to be successful. 'No man is an island' is very true in my case."

He told me he has a lot of mentors he looks up to, views his board of directors "as a guiding light," and also credits his wife of twenty-five years, Ching Sy, as "a vital part of [his] success," noting, "If you have someone you can rely on when you get back at home, tired from work, it energizes you to fight on the next day."

⤺⤻

Toward the end of our conversation, Steve again mentioned his near-disaster with the debt he found himself in all those years ago, which was because, he explained, of his "very high appetite for risk." That comes from God, he believes, who he views as having given him a lot of resources to work with ("To whom much is given…").

Steve thinks of that high-risk tolerance in two ways: as either an opportunity or a temptation. The key, he explained, is discerning which one it is in a given situation, because both of them look good on the outside.

"I think as you grow in age, you learn how to say no to some opportunities because it's really a temptation," he noted. "And that's how I view life. That's how I know, in terms of making the decisions, whether it's going to be good for the company, good for our mission, good for our values."

Where he raised his risk-taking levels even further is with hiring, after seeing the impact it had on the organization. "This investment in top people will create higher value in our company," he explained. "And I learned that when I started hiring more equipped, higher-value people in my organization. That's also why the company grew significantly."

Ultimately, Steve's career and company exist in the volatile e-commerce space, so he's had to refine his adaptability quotient in order to keep changing; it's ironically the only way to stay the course (when it comes to his bigger vision, about which, as I've described, he is deeply committed).

It's about building the right foundation, he told me, adding, "Then the challenge of leadership is to be able to support your team in good times and bad and point them toward the future. Also, when you've gone through a lot of adversity, you become stronger as an organization."

Steve continued, "You develop resilience with adversity in your life. I think those are wonderful years of learning to develop your character, to persevere, to be more persistent, because you know there's a light at the end of the tunnel."

Ultimately for him, success and his faith are inextricably intertwined. "A person can be successful, but at the same time, after a few months, they can be a failure," Steve mused. "So success is just an event for me. What's truly important is following God's will in your life, being faithful to his call—I would say *that's* success."

I'm not personally religious, but I couldn't help but be moved by Steve's conviction. And the fact that Great Deals is so incredibly successful is a testament to that faith.

KEY INSIGHTS:
STEVE AS A FOUNDER WITH CONVICTION

» *Seek higher ground.* For Steve, this showed up specifically as religious faith and a belief in God and the power of prayer. For others, this can appear in a variety of ways, but all of them center on seeing the bigger picture of life and generally operating for the greater good.

» *Find a way to become mission-driven.* Great Deals' company mission is lofty: to uplift Filipino lives. But even for non-founders, studies have shown that having a purpose-driven life is critical to overall health and wellness—of the mental, physical, and emotional variety. Steve's personal and professional mission literally keeps him going.

» ***Stay the course.*** Adversity challenges conviction, and every founder and every person on earth faces it. The key is understanding there is what Steve calls "the light at the end of the tunnel" and recognizing, as he has along the way, that "this too shall pass," and we'll come out on the other side stronger.

CHAPTER 9

ISRAEL AND
THE WEST BANK

My last trip, before the COVID-19 pandemic temporarily stopped me from my typical near-constant travel, was to the Middle East, including Israel. I'd gotten a call from Hilla Brenner, who was the Managing Director of the Techstars Tel Aviv program (the same job I'd had in New York until 2022), asking if I could join her "screening committee," a tradition at the company where other tenured MDs gather for two days to meet the current applicants and help select the most promising companies.

Whenever Hilla would call, I was happy to jump on a plane; I'd helped with her selection committee before, mentored her portfolio companies, and at times, would go and speak to her cohort or sit in on the various programs she organized. As her profile at the end of this chapter will show in more detail, she is just the warmest and most dynamic person, really different from many of the tech founders and funders that I work with. She felt like a family member.

Hilla had solicited a few of my favorite MDs from the US and UK to join her selection committee that year, which made saying yes even easier. The day itself is long, intense, and exhausting, with upwards of twenty-five companies pitching for spots in the program.

To thank us, Hilla promised an amazing cultural excursion the day after the selection committee. Hospitality and being welcoming (not to mention being grateful for our hard work) is just her style, plus she was so proud of her country and wanted all of us to see the beauty and not just the geopolitical issues that receive more attention in the media.

⊱⊰

The Techstars office in Tel Aviv was perfectly situated on the famed Rothschild Boulevard, which is home to many of the startups in the city and lined with the Ficus trees found all around the Mediterranean. The street was one of the first four built in Tel Aviv when Israel became a country, and it's named after Edmond James de Rothschild, a member of the famous banking family who was known for his support of Israel. On breaks between meetings with founders, I'd sneak out of the office to roam the Boulevard and revel in the particular energy of that street.

I've been traveling to the country for years, mainly with a professional focus on the thriving tech sector. Being a global tech investor means spending time in Israel, also known as "The Startup Nation," with its disproportionately high number of successful startups and tech innovations per capita. In fact, Tel Aviv University is ranked first outside the US in the number of unicorn companies established by alumni.

The reality is that Israelis don't build companies for Israel, they build for the rest of the world. With a population of only nine million, the market is too insignificant to build a truly successful venture-scale company, so founders there need to excel at international expansion. While most small and midsize companies hesitate to expand abroad due to competition from multinational corporations and local players, many Israeli companies have figured out how to globalize and become significant players in their industries. In this sense, the country itself has an Everywhere Mindset!

These companies focus on markets and regions over-looked by multinationals and not adequately addressed by local firms—many times thought of as unattractive to the big players. A few examples like Netafim in drip irrigation, Teva Pharmaceutical in generic drugs, and Amdocs in telecommunications billing automation all demonstrate how Israeli firms leveraged their expertise and innovation to enter and dominate global markets.

It's truly mind-bending to witness a country the size of the state of Connecticut acting as such a powerhouse when it comes to innovation—the entire country is focused in that direction. I've had meals with families where a grandparent, a parent, and a child sitting around the same dinner table are all tech entrepreneurs, and it's totally normal, though I guess that makes sense; Israel is a "newer" country in the grand scheme of things, in the same way that tech as we know it is today.

While Israel is well known to be a leader in everything related to cybersecurity, the truth is that they excel across verticals like fintech, healthtech, agritech, and artificial intelligence, among others. Each time I visit, I try to understand more about the drivers of the country's entrepreneurial instincts, wading through all of the complexity and nuance there. Over the years, I've noted that the thriving Israeli tech scene seems to pull elements from its history, culture, the military, robust government programs, and more broadly, its geopolitics.

Israel has mandatory military service, which of course creates a structure that encourages things like problem-solving and working within complex and diverse team dynamics. Plus, I learned from Hilla and others that many people who enlist in the Israeli army receive specialized training that often has a tech component. The most well-known elite military unit is called 8200, and if you're meeting with technical startup founders, you're bound to hear they were part of 8200, similar to the way Harvard grads always seem to work that into any first meeting.

The fact that many women also serve in the Israeli army (like Hilla) as a matter of course, gives the country a foundation of strong women (like Hilla) in business and beyond.

There's a culture of risk-taking that's at play there (Hilla shared much more about this with me in the conversation we had for her adjacent *Venture Everywhere* profile), supported by government grants and policies, as well as programs that attract foreign investors like me. An Israeli friend described it to me in a sobering way: "When a mundane activity like getting on a bus can be a risk [because of terrorism], your perception of risk changes, and your appetite increases out of necessity."

Yet, despite that risk, one of the most interesting things about visiting Israel as a foreigner is how day-to-day safe you feel there in the midst of such an intense and hostile regional environment (noting, of course, that the trip I'm highlighting in this chapter falls before the attacks of October 7, 2023, and the ensuing bloodshed).

During one trip, I was staying near the Carmel Market (the Shuk Ha'Carmel) and found myself walking home by myself at 1:00 a.m. through the dark and very creepy market stalls (think stray cats and overripe fruit squishing under your feet). I would never do this in most other cities, but in Tel Aviv, my perception of danger is either huge or really non-existent: you don't worry so much about being mugged in Israel, but you may worry about your bus being bombed. It's a different type of threat than we typically feel here in the US (though, of course, we in America are not immune to terrorism either).

৵৬

My trip to help Hilla was successful—we'd selected a super strong class of founders and companies—so then it was time for our cultural excursion to Jerusalem to visit the old city and explore. A number of the other MDs had never been to Jerusalem, and some had never been to Israel at all, so for me, it was extra moving to see the city through their eyes.

The mix of cultures we all saw there was nothing short of astounding. We went into the Church of the Holy Sepulchre (recognized as the place where Jesus was crucified, buried, and rose from the dead), ate mind-blowing hummus in the old city, and visited a vineyard, which was Hilla's favorite in the area.

Several times during our trip, Hilla expressed her wish to bring together entrepreneurs and investors from different backgrounds and faiths to help create a dialogue of understanding and empathy. And in a small way, she was doing just that, by gathering this particular group of MDs who were a mix of Hindu, Christian, Catholic, Jewish, and atheist, for a cultural excursion.

Jerusalem is so special because it's a holy land for basically everyone. Jewish people, Christians, and Muslims alike all find the power in it; even non-religious folks were in awe, seeing some of the places that they'd learned about in history books and religious texts as iconic throughout the ages.

It is well known that the name "Jerusalem" in Hebrew translates to "city of peace," but as we wandered through the city, we could all feel the tension based on the long-standing dispute between opposing groups that claim Jerusalem as their capital city. Despite this, one of the most amazing things is the cultural immersion you get in the old city of Jerusalem where everyone lives and worships almost on top of each other.

And the idea about business bringing people together feels particularly synergistic with the next part of my trip, which was into the West Bank in the Palestinian territory—a place where most American tourists certainly don't get to visit. In my case, I've had the opportunity to visit twice and saw its development over a period of about a decade, which was monumental.

My first trip to the West Bank was just about ten years ago as part of a UK tech leaders delegation when I was working for the BBC. One of the top execs at the BBC was supposed to go on the trip, but a few days before, I got the call I got many times, so I was on the next flight to Israel. The purpose of the delegation was to forge closer relationships with media leaders in the UK and Israel more generally, so we spent a week on a bus meeting with top politicians, business and tech leaders, and cultural folks as well.

As part of the trip, they took us to the West Bank to meet with the latest tech company at the time, which was PalTel, the mobile phone company. I remember being in the building and eating in the office cafeteria, which served one type of (unfamiliar) meat and one starch—not the usual massive selection I'm used to at the Google-plex! But the lack of variety was overshadowed by the people there, who were *so* warm and welcoming, and there were many women in the meetings, which was unexpected; for some reason, I assumed PalTel would be dominated by men, perhaps tracking with my vision of how corporate America operated in earlier eras. But that was not my experience at all, and I was pleasantly surprised about the diversity of the organization (at least as presented to our group).

At the time, Ramallah was still rather rural-looking compared to Tel Aviv where we were staying. The land was arid and dusty, and we saw animals roaming the side of the roads. In town, there were a few buildings, but they were interspersed with open lots and overgrown flora.

The second time I journeyed to the West Bank was during the summer of 2023 to meet with local founders and the one venture fund based there, Ibtikar Fund, which is run by Ambar Amleh (a Kauffman Fellows classmate), who is an amazing human. She's doing something *really* hard, namely bringing capital to local entrepreneurs in a highly unstable region.

It was notable to me that, during my first trip to the West Bank, there weren't tech startups to speak of, so instead, we visited that mobile phone provider I mentioned along with a media company, which were essentially the closest alternatives. Ten years later, we were meeting with actual startups, not corporations—what a (major) difference a decade makes!

It takes a *lot* to build a company in the West Bank—the territory has a very small population, so founders have to be building regionally at minimum. Many of the founders living there had lived in Jordan or in places like the UAE or the US, so they had a more global point of view and experience with bigger markets. They understood they couldn't just build for their small community. They needed to build for a larger Middle Eastern platform. And like many emerging markets, the startups we met primarily focused on fintech, infrastructure, and logistics.

The burgeoning West Bank scene was super interesting and very inspiring to me—I was meeting startups that felt familiar, more like those I would meet in the US. Plus, the presence of Ambar's venture fund was a testament that there was capital and resources going to these founders. So not only were they doing it, they were doing it in a scalable way, extra impressive given the limitations there.

The West Bank is not very accessible. While different passport holders have different access options, in general, traveling in and out requires paperwork as well a local connection that can assess the safety in the area during that moment in time. That restrictiveness definitely includes the people who live there and also can't come and go very easily. There are sixty-three gates at the West Bank barrier into Israel, of which half are available for Palestinian use; however, all Palestinians are required to have a permit to cross.

So, if you live in the West Bank, for example, you can't just head to the airport at will like those of us who travel constantly do without giving it a second thought.

Israel's Ben Gurion is the closest airport, requiring a forty-five-minute drive to the Qalandia checkpoint. Queen Alia International Airport in Amman, Jordan, is an hour to the King Hussein (better known as the Allenby Bridge) checkpoint, but someone hoping to get across can expect up to three hours of queuing and completing all security checks in order to do so. There are no last-minute sprints to airports when you live in the West Bank if you happen to be running late. Everything must be planned well in advance.

A lot of the Palestinians I met go through Jordan to get to the airport as a workaround; they fly into Jordan, then take a ride-share into the West Bank, where they pick up their car, which they'd left on that side of the border.

But beyond that mind-blowingly complex manner of travel, the development and modernization of the West Bank I saw during my second journey there was notable.

When I went to Ramallah on the more recent trip, it was pretty incredible how much new infrastructure there was, coupled with so many buildings and so much life in town. It felt very vibrant. Ramallah was much more built up with proper high-rises, office buildings, and general modernization, and the most obvious sign of progress there was that the center was totally bustling with people—a sharp contrast to when I saw it the first time.

On the 2023 trip, I didn't feel like anyone noticed my presence as anything abnormal as I walked through town—I can pass for a few different nationalities, but it's usually the clothing that gives me away as an American—and I felt much more comfortable fitting in. Ten years prior, had I taken a stroll around town, I would've stood out starkly, mainly because there just wasn't much there at all, including many paved roads or the other markers of contemporary, urban life. Today, it's no longer an off-roading experience; it feels like a true, buzzing city center.

We had a delicious lunch at a local Palestinian restaurant (with lots of variation in the cuisine) and took a walk to a spot to sample their famous ice cream (it was tasty but chewier than I was used to), then headed over to Ibtikar, the local venture capital fund, to meet some founders. Although I felt totally connected to these founders because we're all working in tech, sometimes they would say things that would be jarring to me. For example, instead of saying an "Israeli person said this," they would say, "The *occupier* said this." It reminded me that, as hopeful as I am about the potential for entrepreneurship to bring people together in incredibly creative and fruitful ways, you can only keep politics out of things for so long, and progress, while underway, is still a long road.

CONVICTION, as it appears again here, is less about the bigger-picture purpose (and/or specific religious belief) and more about being positive and trusting the inner voice. Also, it's a reminder that, while conviction often presents all at once as a strong preference or direction, in reality, people build conviction over time as they gather data, insights, and experiences.

CONVICTION IN ACTION:

» *Take calculated risks.* Probably nothing is riskier than traveling to a war-torn region, but I've always felt the pull to travel around the Middle East. I weighed the risk for what I believed in, then pushed ahead to travel to both Israel and the West Bank multiple times, regardless of the risk (though still respecting it).

» **_Build bridges._** Actively bringing people together who, at first glance, might have no common ground like Hilla did on our trip to Jerusalem—a city that is the crossroads for many disparate religions and cultures and a hotbed of discord as different groups vie for "ownership" over it. I did this myself in this region by making sure I visited both Israel and the West Bank (since for me it happened to be possible); yes, it was in the context of business, but connecting the dots benefits everyone, especially builders like me.

» **_Going against the grain._** Having, not to mention maintaining, your conviction at any given time can be challenging based on the circumstances. At some point, I felt that the Israeli startup scene had gotten out of balance with too much capital-chasing and too few deals. As such, startup valuations skyrocketed, and my fund was essentially priced out of the market. I suspected this was temporary and a correction was inevitable, so I paused on investing into Israeli companies despite continuing to travel to Israel and the region. At that point, I got pushback from colleagues and other investors about whether I was making the right decision for myself and my fund. Luckily, the entire tech world has equalized, and I'm excited to be investing in companies in the region once again. Staying on course ironically means sometimes swimming upriver or climbing uphill!

HILLA BRENNER, FOUNDER OF WHITESMOKE

If I had to name a superpower of Hilla Brenner, founder of grammar and writing software company WhiteSmoke (and now an investor in tech startups), it's optimism. And it's infectious—when you talk with her, even when she's relaying challenging, scary, or really bad times or experiences, she has a smile on her face that makes you feel like everything is going to be okay.

"Optimistic people are more successful because they enjoy what they do more," she opined during our conversation." Later on, she also told me that, to her, success means "To be happy and start the day with a smile on your face."

Of course, it's not like Hilla hasn't had her challenges, some self-imposed and some coming from the outside world. Her family is Israeli but had moved to South Africa when she and her siblings were young. Hilla was intrigued by her heritage, though, and came to Israel on her own when she turned eighteen, where she promptly fell in love with everything about the country.

Not only did she decide to stay permanently (much to her family's shock) but she also immediately volunteered for the Israeli Defense Forces (IDF), which added another layer to her love of her adopted country. She told me she got a huge amount of support from the Israeli army during her time as an enlistee, but maybe more importantly, she said she learned a lot about resilience and about "doing things with a really strong passion."

Her worldview firmly implanted, post-army Hilla got a first and second degree in law and intended to focus on a career in human rights. But once again, the country of Israel drew her in a different direction, this time toward entrepreneurship. Her then-boyfriend (now husband) was working for a company called ICQ, which was one of Israel's first big startup success stories, selling for $500 million. I knew of that company before I ever met Hilla and knew having a front row seat to that kind of startup excitement changed the game for her and her life trajectory.

There's something else about Hilla as a startup founder that I find really interesting: she didn't have a big idea or a major problem to solve that was plaguing her, which is how many founders come to the table. Instead, she loved and felt so at home in the vibrant entrepreneurial environment in Israel, and *that* was what urged her to start a business.

"It felt like both my army service and the Israeli ecosystem around me were urging people to take risks and be creative and start their own thing," she told me. "I realized there was something about risk-taking in this environment that was just something that people thought was acceptable. And I think that's probably why there's so many startups here too."

So Hilla jumped right into it—but she was quick to remind me that it's not necessarily about the idea itself (especially because she decided to become an entrepreneur before she had a viable one) but about the passion behind it.

"I was walking around for weeks thinking, *What's my idea going to be?*" Hilla said with a laugh. "Now, I always say to entrepreneurs, you don't really have to have a perfect idea. You just have to be super passionate."

At the time, her passion was rooted in writing, which she loved to do. She was also a lawyer by training and knew a lot of other Israeli lawyers who wanted to improve their English writing skills. That's when she landed on how she wanted to change the world, and the first version of WhiteSmoke was born: an AI (before AI was a thing!) English-language grammar and learning tool.

Many years later, WhiteSmoke was living on over 50 million computers, was licensed by Pearson Education, and won a prestigious Product of the Year award.

But of course, that didn't happen overnight, and Hilla had to jump over hurdles that I have seen many good entrepreneurs back down from without a fight. First was fundraising, which was "hell" for her in the beginning. "I had no experience," Hilla said. "I didn't know anything about it, my presentations were not so great, my pictures were not so great, nothing." But luckily, she loved going to meetings and connecting with people, another natural skill she has that can be super taxing for different, less extroverted founders. And that optimism of hers never waned until eventually, as people writing the checks started to get to know her, everything became easier, including raising capital.

That is, until three years into the company's operations.

When she started WhiteSmoke, Hilla envisioned it as a tool for non-native English speakers. Since that iteration of the product was selling "by the millions," she told me she thought her company was "the greatest thing since sliced bread."

Except focus group after focus group showed that the tool resonated with many more native English speakers—particularly students—than non-native speakers (think Chinese, Japanese, Italians, etc.).

That turned the company's entire go to market strategy upside down—in fact, it changed everything.

But before Hilla accepted that, she obstinately stuck to the paradigm she'd started on—adamant that she knew what she was doing—and kept raising money on the old story. She had tunnel vision *for* her vision.

"I was making that same mistake of looking at the problem space through my own eyes and being in love with my solution and being in love with the market that I thought was a great market," she told me ruefully. "So, in particular, my story tells another story of how you should really listen to other people and how it can change your strategy."

She continued, "Many entrepreneurs just don't think big enough, and they don't open a wide enough window. That was something I think I did do correctly; right from the beginning, I wanted to be very global, but I didn't really understand my market well enough."

I can totally understand how a first-time founder would trip up and ultimately learn that understanding a market and a strategy for launching a product in it are critical to focus on—I've seen it many times before, along with founders who persist in being perhaps a little too stubborn for a little too long when the time to make a pivot becomes apparent.

With Hilla, though, I was also curious about a corollary challenge, one which I myself have personally faced: being a woman in tech and the startup world. I asked her if she purposefully put on that tough, unwavering exterior in order to make her own way among the majority—men.

"Yes," she agreed, "I was trying to look really strong, and I was trying to be very confident and look like I knew what I was doing because of how the world looks at you when you're young, when you're inexperienced, and when you're a woman."

She went on to say, "But on the other hand, I think it's giving me a little bit too much leeway here, because in general, I was a little too picky. So today, I know that it makes you much stronger if you actually do listen. And so, if I look back at my younger self, I think I would have told myself to listen more."

Then there was the experience of wanting—and trying hard—to take WhiteSmoke public in the vaunted US market. But unfavorable market conditions coupled with WhiteSmoke's financial results made the proposition of going public on the Nasdaq a tough one. In short, she failed.

According to *Forbes*, of the 6,117 companies that have gone public since the year 2000, only forty of them were led by women, less than twenty-five of which were founded *solely* by a woman or women.

Also, we all know the dismal stats on startups in general: 90 percent of them fail, and of the 10 percent that make it, only a small sliver are able to take their companies public. In 2012, the year Hilla tried to take WhiteSmoke public, 157 companies went public. Taking a startup public is not something you just decide to do, there's a year of prep—leveling up the team, getting financials to a good place, and ultimately telling the right story to the market.

Even with that knowledge, "I was devastated," Hilla told me, and I could still see the disappointment on her face when she talked about it. But once again, the country of Israel proved to be her anchor. Her investors insisted on taking the IPO back to Israel, and though she was emotional about not getting it done where and how she wanted to, it became another success story in Israel.

Hearing all the nitty-gritty around her experiences and how she thought about and got through them made me see that Hilla's self-awareness and self-acceptance, along with her optimism, all paint the bigger picture of her conviction. At one point during our conversation, she told me a story about toting her three-week-old daughter around New York City—where it was about seventeen degrees at the time—in order to raise money from investors there.

"I said to myself, I'm a different kind of mom, and I have to be happy with it," Hilla said, with a shrug and a smile. She knew she'd have to make sacrifices—contrary to popular (patriarchal?) belief, you can't "have it all," but Hilla found a way to marry the personal and professional in a way that works for her and allows her to quickly turn challenges into opportunities.

"Optimism really gives me more and more—it makes it easier for me to overcome [challenges] and to actually deal with them. So, for me, it's also a tool," she explained.

Hilla's huge vision is so apparent, and while it's framed by her big belief and passion and love for what she's doing, it's grounded in changing the world, even when things were bad or when she experienced failures.

She was also, of course, devastated by the events of October 7, 2023, and felt her beloved country of Israel would be forever changed, but Hilla, as always, holds out hope for a better future. "We need to make this world a better place," she told me firmly. "I think if the world was led by women, it would be a better place. Also, if entrepreneurs got together from different regions, even today, from Gaza and from Israel, then I think things would look different. I'm a great believer in putting the regions together and getting people that are more oriented to human rights and making this world a better place to connect with each other."

Ultimately, Hilla's conviction lies in the idea that entrepreneurship (and women) truly can save the world, and since the day I met her, that's a vision I've been able to easily get behind.

KEY INSIGHTS:
HILLA AS A FOUNDER WITH CONVICTION

» *Fall in love.* Hilla fell head over heels for the country of Israel (to the point where she volunteered to join the military). There, she found her professional calling as a successful founder and also met her future husband. Passion and conviction usually go hand-in-hand, so start with a bit of love and excitement and watch how things blossom from there.

» *There is such a thing as too much conviction.* Hilla described how she held on to the early vision/model for her company for too long, and in the process, prolonged her path to success and made things more challenging for herself along the way. Having conviction should not preclude being malleable and open to new ways of doing things.

» *Entrepreneurship can change the world.* Like Hilla espoused (and like I've seen time and time again with the companies I've invested in and also with the smallest of local businesses, like a bodega in Barcelona or a scuba diving company in the Philippines), they are solving a problem or bridging a divide and changing the world for the better at the same time.

CHAPTER 10

BRAZIL

I flew into Sao Paulo in April 2023 for a few days before heading to Rio de Janeiro to speak at Web Summit, the European tech conference that was making its Latin-American debut. The startup scene in Brazil is centered in Sao Paulo, and it was just the excuse I needed to get back there to catch up with some of the founders my fund, Everywhere Ventures, had invested in and to meet new ones we might back in the future.

One investing principle I take to places like Brazil is teaming up with the "smart money" on the ground—i.e., the venture capitalists who've been sweating it out for years there, helping to build the ecosystem from the ground up. I also ended each VC meeting with the same question: *Who is the most unique early-stage founder that I need to meet while I'm here?* This helps me organically build my list of companies and contacts.

One of my favorite on-the-ground visits during that particular trip was with Marcelo Lima, a partner at monashees, one of the most well established and active venture capital funds in the region. After an intense day of meetings, I showed up at their office (which was, incidentally, located in an area of Sao Paulo called "Novo Brooklin"—hilarious to me, because by now, you're familiar with my quirky, Brooklynite grandparents and their oversized influence on my life).

I knew Marcelo was a wine guy, witnessing him in the past crossing multiple continents with his favorite bottles lovingly wrapped in his suitcases and checked to his final destination. He was not at all concerned that the airline might lose his clothing and other belongings, but he was *very* worried they would lose his precious wine! So, I wasn't surprised when he ushered me into a small conference room to show off his wine refrigerator. I mentally prepared myself for the extensive tasting that was sure to come.

I was surprised, though, and very touched, when things went in a different direction, and he told me about the origins of the particular bottles he was showing me. When monashees backs a new founder with an investment, they buy two bottles of the same wine; monashees keeps one, and they give the other to the founder. The bottles are saved, and once the company has exited successfully, they celebrate by opening the now-aged wine and toasting to the years of hard work they'd engaged in together.

That experience only underscored the magic I found in Brazil, which originated even before I'd actually been to the country. My interest in (and excitement for) it began when I was a young child, and my mother started a business with an eccentric woman named Marga. Her ancestors were also originally from Eastern Europe, and when they fled persecution, instead of coming through Ellis Island like my family did, they landed in Brazil. Because of that, her entry in my life always seemed star-crossed in a way—she beguiled me—and I always thought about how different my life would be if our family had taken a different boat. That (and Marga herself) is definitely the reason why Brazil has a deeply-rooted place in my imagination and in my heart.

That probably set the stage for my appreciation of Brazil from a cultural perspective, beyond my business trips. A number of times, I found myself wandering—and getting lost, but not minding at all—in the super-buzzy Jardins area. Brazil has a unique culinary culture as well; it has the largest population of Japanese people outside of Japan, and as a result, it has some of the best Japanese food and restaurants in the world, making it a mecca for a sushi-lover like me. A lot of these restaurants are situated in Jardins, which is why I was so reluctant to find my way out of that area!

When I told folks I was going to Brazil, everyone seemed to have a relevant connection for me to track down there, so my trip to Sao Paulo was packed. One of our portfolio founders Dave (whose company Ned we had invested in at Everywhere Ventures), had a Brazilian angel investor on his capitalization table—a retired corporate executive who now ran an informal angel investing group. Dave wanted me to meet him.

I went to meet this investor at his office (where he chastised me for walking the streets of São Paulo alone, though the New Yorker in me didn't think a thing about it, especially in broad daylight), expecting to have a one-on-one, but six other angel investors were sitting around the spacious conference room table, eager to meet me. Our casual meet-and-greet turned into more of a presentation about my fund and a thesis on trends in tech, which I wasn't quite expecting—but those angels couldn't have been more lovely and welcoming, and after we met, they were so excited to share deals.

As I was leaving, I noticed a mezuzah (Hebrew for "doorpost"—a piece of parchment inscribed with specific Hebrew verses from the Torah, which Jewish people often affix to the doorposts of their homes) on the door of the entryway, and that made me pause and take a second look. Growing up in New York City, it was quite common to see these lining the doorframes of apartments, offices, and even hospital rooms, but I didn't expect to see one in Brazil; even though there is a large population of Jews there, it's still a predominantly Catholic country. One of the guys in the meeting explained that the angel investor was Jewish, and he maintained that tradition. It felt like a little bit of home right there in São Paulo.

After that manic day of meeting with investors, I was definitely ready for our evening activity—a mixer with local founders. I teamed up with Laura Constantini from Astella, one of the long standing and well-respected seed funds in the city, to gather the local startup community. Laura arranged for a fun venue, and somehow, our little gathering bloomed into a larger party after founders in the ecosystem heard about it and just showed up.

When you're in Brazil, you feel the pull of community and how much Brazilians enjoy congregating and bringing people together—it's a deeply entrenched part of the culture, which spills over into tech, where founders seem like family with one another. A real warmth can be felt at these gatherings, and I was greeted with open arms and, of course, kisses: Brazilians kiss people they are meeting (even for the first time) at least two or three times!

Parties and culture and people aside, the ever-growing contingent of startups and VCs in Brazil, particularly in São Paulo, have a nearly mystical power all its own. The country's startup ecosystem has taken flight, fueled by a surge in entrepreneurial activity, increased venture capital dollars, and a relatively supportive regulatory environment. Like many emerging markets, Brazil's fintech sector was among the first to flourish, addressing gaps in traditional financial services. There has also been a significant expansion of the e-commerce sector, driven by the growing middle class and increased Internet penetration.

Another fascinating sociological component of every locality I travel to is the differences in the local venture capitalists. One of the things I most admire about the VCs I know in Brazil is how dedicated they are to the profession and their firms. It's not uncommon for them to be working as a VC at the same firm for a decade or more. In a profession where there seems to be a lot of hopping around and flipping back and forth from operator to founder to funder in the US, it was refreshing to see a different model and level of commitment.

ꕔꕔ

I left São Paulo forty-eight hours after landing, continuing on to the storied Rio de Janeiro and the conference I was speaking at.

I'd not yet been to Rio and had heard different things from different people, but looking out the airplane window at the white sand beaches and the view of the famed Sugarloaf Mountain, I knew that it was my place...or one of them, at least!

Going to tech conferences is like being on tour with your favorite rock band. There's a core group (if not groupies) that migrates loosely together from event to event, only we're fans of product, good user interface, and artificial intelligence—not the Stones or the Dead—and we carry adapters and USB cables and blue-light glasses instead of joints and aviator sunglasses.

Arriving a day early in Rio meant I had a day to explore and check out the town with my conference crew.

One of my exploring companions was Itxaso del Palacio, a general partner at Notion Capital, who has more energy and enthusiasm than just about any VC I know. She had just flown in from London and was also eager to explore, so off we went to Sugarloaf and the statue of Christ the Redeemer on top of Corcovado, which are two of the top attractions in Rio. It was a beautiful day so we braved the lines, but after waiting thirty minutes and not moving an inch, two type-A VCs had had enough and promptly figured out how to buy VIP passes online (the website was entirely in Portuguese I might add) to circumvent the line. Next thing you know, we were in a cushy room with air conditioning, then being escorted into a cable car to ascend the mountain.

Our next stop was a late lunch in Ipanema with Zach Coelius (from Coelius Capital in San Francisco) and friends he'd made while running a startup with offices in Rio. Zach is always up for adventures, and I'd met up with him over the years in various places like Portugal, Saudi Arabia, and now Rio. At this point we were starving, and Zach escorted us to the exact right place—a fun Brazilian-meets-Californian cafe called Zaza Bistro, where we over-ordered and enjoyed lively conversation in multiple languages as more friends and friends of friends joined our table.

We finished everything off, then grabbed ice cream and headed to the beach as the sun was setting, exactly what I was told *not* to do (that is, walking on the beach after dark). It was amazing. And remember, I had my trusty crew with me, so I wasn't venturing alone.

The last stop of the evening was at a party hosted by one of the local investors at his flat across the street from the beach. There, we ran into a bunch of other American and European conference-goers and a few local founders. On the balcony overlooking the sea, I started chatting with Rafael Duton, co-founder of the 21212 Digital Accelerator, which launched in 2011 with the goal of helping entrepreneurs create value in the Brazilian digital market.

He reminded me that Brazil's startup scene was a "fifteen-year overnight success."

I know from being both a founder and VC that those "overnight success" stories are almost always a mirage, and a number of my founder profiles in *Venture Everywhere* demonstrate that, often in stark detail. But that moment was a good reminder for me from one of the smartest people in the Brazilian startup scene.

The day of the conference dawned. It was the first year that this particular conference, well known in Europe, had decided to set up in Brazil, tapping into the energy and excitement around Brazil's burgeoning tech ecosystem. And although most startups and VCs are based in São Paulo, the appeal of Rio as a destination was undeniable, if for nothing other than its breathtaking beauty.

I'd been tasked by the conference organizers to assemble a panel of industry experts to talk about the shifting nature of funding for early-stage founders. I picked some of my favorite local VCs and added in my global explorer friend Zach, who is notorious for having strong opinions with little filter, to keep things interesting.

At one point on the second day of the conference, I was sharing the main stage in front of thousands of people with the storied third-generation venture capitalist Tim Draper, who started the firm DFJ and famously paid $19 million for 30,000 Bitcoin that had been seized from the Silk Road Exchange by the US Marshal service and auctioned to the public.

After a lively discussion, out of the blue, Tim decided to stand up, walk to the mic and break out into a totally impromptu rap song about his life and enthusiasm for Bitcoin. The rest of the speakers were all stunned into silence, and the audience (remember, lots of tech nerds who don't like surprises) stared, shocked.

Never a dull moment in startup land.

No dull moments in the Brazilian startup scene at all, in fact. My growing excitement for business there was only bolstered after everything I saw and experienced in both São Paulo and Rio, despite the current tech slowdown.

The country is one of the most connected digital markets in the world with super high mobile penetration, though, despite this connectivity, it's also extremely bureaucratic and riddled with structural inefficiencies. Obviously, this is not great for the people who live there, but it does present serious opportunities for entrepreneurs looking to solve problems and remove friction.

Since the last time I visited, companies like Nubank, an innovative digital bank, have gained prominence and achieved unicorn status, signaling the disruption of the traditional banking industry. Platforms like MercadoLibre have played pivotal roles in shaping Brazil's digital retail landscape, proptech startups like Loft, to healthcare solutions like Sami (this chapter's profile is Sami's founder Vitor Asseituno) have all come to the forefront, working valiantly to create a brighter future for the country.

KINETIC's second appearance in *Venture Everywhere* signifies not just physical energy and stamina but being a fast thinker—Kinetics in this context respond quickly and decisively to issues and events. They also excitedly and energetically explore the world around them, gaining even more inspiration from their environment and experiences in it, plus the people they find there.

KINETIC IN ACTION:

» *Cultivate community.* This might be one of the most important takeaways for both business and life, and it's something kinetics—usually pretty charismatic people—do really well. This showed up in Brazil when we hosted a casual mixer that became the destination event of the evening, or when I gathered friends in Rio (from all around the world) for a day of exploration. Especially for an introvert like me, it's important to continue to forge connections with new people, because that, in and of itself, creates powerful and productive energy.

> » *Think fast and act faster.* Just like we did when we were faced with an hours-long line on our day of exploring Sugarloaf Mountain in Rio, find a way to make yourself a VIP (even if you're technically not yet designated as one!) to get where you want to go.

> » *All who wander...* The French call this being a "flaneur," and I can't think of anything more kinetic than doing things like roaming the streets of São Paulo and strolling through Jardins (where I discovered amazing Japanese food, among a hundred other things). There is tremendous kinetic energy unearthed by exploring the unknown.

VITOR ASSEITUNO, CO-FOUNDER OF SAMI

It's hard for me to remember if Vitor invested in our fund, Everywhere Ventures, or if we invested in his company, Sami, a Brazil-based digital healthcare company, first—that's the kind of unique relationship we have.

Everywhere Ventures is backed by 500 founders and operators who make up our limited partner (LP) base, so part of our secret sauce is that we get access to our LPs' companies when they go out to raise capital before other VCs do.

Even without our intermingled backstory, though, Vitor's energy is infectious, and our conversation for this book could've gone on for hours; I wasn't surprised when he told me that, during his first trip to Silicon Valley years ago, after only two weeks, he had already connected with and knew the majority of the investors living there.

Part of that was learning that Silicon Valley is basically just a few small cities, not the center of the universe (which might surprise people because it's painted in such mythic proportions outside of the startup world), but it also says a lot about

Vitor's ability to tap into the heart of people, communicate, and bring people together.

He was born in a small town in the countryside outside São Paulo, Brazil, but his ambition blossomed at a really young age, when he discovered a copy of *Forbes* at a family friend's house. This was followed quickly by other "light reading" by Stephen Covey, Jack Welch, and Peter Drucker; from there, he became fascinated with things like management, mergers and acquisitions, and sales. Not your average pre-teen hobbies!

At seventeen, Vitor went to medical school, but not before learning how to code, setting the stage for his future company at the important intersection of tech, management, and health.

I've always been curious if this kind of early ambition is something innate or if it's a nurture thing. Vitor told me that, in his case, it's a result of his high self-esteem, which his mom cultivated in him. "No matter where you come from, you can do something big," Vitor told me. "And that is about self-esteem. Just give me some time and money. We can make anything happen."

"But high self-esteem can also be a trap," he continued with a rueful smile, adding, "I'm working through that with my coach now! I'm learning that sometimes you're so confident you might not hear other people as much as you should."

🐑🐑

In his final year of medical school, Vitor sent a "cold" email that changed his life: he found a contact at Rock Health, the digital health investment firm with a nonprofit arm, and offered to intern there for free, working in the accelerator program. Then he got on a plane to San Francisco and did just that.

This was, to say the least, a nontraditional approach to his education and his path to building companies, which centered on his ability to align with many different types of people–even, and perhaps especially, those he'd never met before and who didn't know him at all.

"For me it strengthened the belief that it's not just about building impactful products; it's equally important to develop a deep network and community," he told me. "As an intern, I was doing things like cleaning desks and organizing demo day, but I was also at the reception desk at demo day, and I exchanged business cards with one hundred VCs in one night."

His experience at Rock Health inspired Vitor to bring community back to Brazil in the (second) biggest way he could: by organizing a digital health conference and trade show—which became a startup he ran for four years and ultimately sold to a public company in London called Informa Group.

By then, Vitor had already started wondering when the digital health boom he was witnessing in the US during his tenure at Rock Health would happen in Brazil. At the time, Brazil was the second-largest global market for Facebook, the second-largest global market for Twitter, the second-largest private healthcare market worldwide, and the country with the second-most medical schools in the world, just behind India. He also learned there was a lack of management in healthcare and medicine overall. "Physicians don't like to manage stuff," he told me. "They like to operate on patients, and usually, businesspeople don't understand medicine and don't understand the healthcare industry."

"I started questioning things that physicians don't usually question," he said. He realized, "There's a special place that I could fit in here."

Brazil has a universal healthcare system, plagued by the same problems other countries with that system face: huge wait times for service, among other things. As a result, a significant number of people buy private insurance, but inflation in the country has caused massive price hikes, which have or will price most people out.

Bottom line, both systems in Brazil have not been able to deliver services at a reasonable price or in a reasonable time frame, which creates a huge gulf…and an opportunity for someone with Vitor's vision.

Vitor was finally ready to tackle this issue, and his background as a doctor, founder of a health conference (not to mention his impressive global network), clearly made him the right person to take on such a highly regulated and complicated startup concept.

I'd, of course, known a lot of this, as Sami is one of our portfolio companies, but in our conversation, Vitor shared more about how he actually did it—and it circles right back to his ability to forge (in a really courageous way) authentic connections.

Like when he reached out to his medical school professor who was, at the time, the CEO of UnitedHealth Brazil (the largest operation of UnitedHealth outside of the US). "I want to build UnitedHealth 2.0 in Brazil," Vitor told him bluntly when he answered the phone. As it turned out, his professor was leaving UnitedHealth for sabbatical and became an important Sami advisor, helping Sami adapt all the learnings and ideas of telemedicine into a "value-based solution."

Being a risk-taker is a typical startup founder characteristic, and Vitor was no different. His interpersonal risks—cold-calling Rock Health, making countless connections with investors, and recruiting a high-level team of advisors and colleagues—have paid off handsomely.

One thing he shared with me that blew my mind, though, was the true financial risk of starting a company in Brazil, where the founder's personal assets are tied directly to the company (unlike, for example, in the US, where founders are protected by LLC structures or other business entities).

"People talk a lot about the perseverance of founders, and I think there is a big inspirational piece to that," he told me. "But for me, there's no ability to 'walk away.' Other people have options. We don't."

When Vitor shared all of this, I thought about what a strong leader he is—*has* to be—so I asked him how he defined leadership.

"There's a quote from a Brazilian business guy that says, 'The leader is the person who delivers results.' That's it," he told me. "So, I don't think you can be an effective leader if you don't deliver results. But being a leader also means guiding and fostering a group to a specific destination and getting there sooner or later with more or less resources. But if we said we're going to get there, we're going to work our best to guide the team to get there."

Even with the (what seems to me unbelievable) pressure of his and his family's financial life being intrinsically entwined with Sami, Vitor doesn't seem fazed, and from my vantage point, he really has been this kind of leader: Sami raised $15.5 million in venture funding in 2020, the largest Series A round on record for a Latin American health startup at the time. They went on to raise additional capital in a Series B transaction in 2023 to scale their platform and implement new technology-based tools.

Maybe it all goes back to his ability to capture and capitalize on energy (or, as I described it earlier, how kinetics like him are able to "manufacture serendipity"). He also told me that someone wrote a recommendation for him on LinkedIn and said, "Vitor was able to speak about his big vision as if it was real and already here."

But really, he said, it starts and ends with his positive mindset, which is based in his religious beliefs. Earlier in our conversation, he'd told me in an aside, "God will take care of things—and me—even when things are awful."

Although I didn't know explicitly about his religious faith before interviewing him, I always had a feeling that Vitor was driven by a higher purpose. His journey has not been easy, and working in healthcare—especially at the scale he is—has constant setbacks, but he is unwavering, energetically drawing toward him the right experiences and people for ultimate success.

KEY INSIGHTS:
VITOR AS A KINETIC FOUNDER

» *In the flow full-throttle.* The truth in startups is that every founder needs to sprint hard for periods of time; it's a common denominator among them. In Vitor's case, he learned how to code, knowing it would come in handy later, applied for an internship, and paid his own way just to get himself to San Francisco. Then, in a flurry, he met a huge percentage of the VCs in Palo Alto in just two weeks.

» *Deliver results.* Vitor's brand of kinetic focuses on leadership as the ability to drive results. In the startup world (and especially in venture-backed startups), though different companies might take different roads, results are the end goal. The good news is, the results themselves will also look very different to each company—but in Vitor's case, being a leader means guiding his team toward a specific destination and getting there sooner or later with more or less resources.

» *Confidence, never arrogance.* I loved that Vitor told me he's working with a coach to mitigate the trap of overly high-self-esteem. Confidence is fundamental in the world of entrepreneurship, but so is listening to other people at the right times and possessing the judgment to know when to take and implement feedback.

CHAPTER 11

KENYA AND NIGERIA

For years, I'd been looking for an excuse to visit Kenya, and I finally had the perfect one with the Kauffman Fellows Global Summit, a four-day gathering with top minds in tech in the local ecosystem (founders and investors) and other business leaders and politicians interested in tech.

The fellowship itself is a two-year program for people who work in venture capital, after which, fellows are able to attend the global summits with Kauffman alumni from all over the world. In 2023, the Global Summit was held in Kenya, an important crossroads for innovation and a growing player in startups, and it was hosted by all the fellows who live and work across Africa at firms such as Atlantica, Norrsken22, Ingressive Capital, Greenhouse Capital, Africa50, and CRE.

The purpose of the summits is to build bridges between the top global investors and the local ecosystem they're hosted in, while also providing tangible impact on the local economy, as the organization has always believed in the power of entrepreneurship as a means for creating local wealth.

A lot of startup energy in Africa originates in Nigeria (including that of Babs Ogundeyi of Kuda Bank, the founder I profile adjacent to this chapter); it's perhaps the most well-known and largest of the startup ecosystems across the region. With a huge (200 million strong!) and diverse population that's open to embracing innovation, the country has seen a surge in ambitious entrepreneurs across various sectors, emerging as a leader in fintech (and financial inclusion) across Africa. It has also seen a ton of growth in other areas like e-commerce, agritech and foodtech, healthcare, and energy tech. All of this gets an assist from the Nigerian government, which has put initiatives in place to support entrepreneurship and innovation, including funding programs, tax incentives, and regulatory reforms.

And, while much of the startup excitement is happening in Nigeria, Kenya is also making rapid progress, as I saw firsthand on my trip there.

My Kenyan adventure started on my very first night with an investor event I attended. The governor was in attendance. As he gave the welcome speech, all I could focus on was how young he looked and how cool his sneakers were—he was nothing like the average US politician I was used to seeing, that's for sure.

While he talked about all the benefits of doing business in Kenya, as any good politician would, one statistic stayed etched in my mind: *the median age in Kenya is just over nineteen and a half years old.* (Compare that to the US where it's thirty-eight years old, or Japan, where it's forty-eight years old). This is significant and presents an undeniable opportunity for local entrepreneurs and innovators, even amidst the challenges that a younger population can pose (including issues around unemployment, education, and maternal healthcare). A low median age offers a bigger and stronger workforce, bolstering economic output, and a younger population can bring more energy, excitement, and creativity—plus a willingness to embrace innovation. And, of course, younger people tend to be more tech-forward.

We also met with the president of the Republic of Kenya, Dr. William Samoei Ruto. His talk focused on his plans to turn Kenya into a financially inclusive economy, utilizing the power of technology and his country's thriving startup ecosystem to foster development.

A corollary thing I noticed on that trip was how integral women were in the tech scene. In fact, Africa has a higher proportion of female general partners and check-writers at venture capital funds than the US does.

These positive stats were underscored for me while attending an inspirational workshop and pitch event for women in tech hosted by Women Who Build Africa (WWBA). WWBA provided a compelling glimpse into the progress that female founders are making and the work the organization is doing to support them across the region. As I mentioned earlier, part of the objective of any Kauffman Summit is connecting people and regions, and it was amazing to see many of the Kaufmann Fellows investors leaning in to learn more about the local startup founders. It's with this better understanding of the vast local opportunities that the region will be able to attract more foreign capital.

Despite all the good news and excitement surrounding the Kenyan tech ecosystems, access to capital is still a challenge for startups. And without capital, things like innovation, growth, and market expansion are all hindered. Similarly, as places like the US and Europe struggle during the tech downturn, Kenya is not immune, also dealing with the fallout from high interest rates and more risk-averse investors.

֍֍

I couldn't visit Africa without exploring the wildlife and natural beauty there, which is really in a class of its own. Although, as I've mentioned, the startup scene in Nigeria is bigger than in Kenya (and more fellows live there), the Kauffman Global Summits are hosted in locations where fellows can do inspirational side trips in addition to Summit events, and that's why we found ourselves in Kenya. Some fellows splintered off to experience the beaches of Lamu, and others, like us, voyaged to the Maasai Mara to go on a safari and stay at Tangulia Mara, the first Maasai-owned and operated lodge.

This was an incredible experience, but perhaps not your everyday safari as I was with a group of fellows (from all over the world), who are all VCs. Our days were spent tracking animals and exploring the off-the-charts beauty of the environment in our jeep, but liberally sprinkled in were intense group shares about deal flow, commiserations about the current tech down-turn, and comparisons of the latest gadgets. You can take the girl out of the VC world....

One day, we visited the local village where the owner and staff of the safari camp originally came from, which was filled with huts called Maasai shelters. These were unusual and really interesting circular or loaf-shaped dwellings, crafted by the women of the tribe.

The Maasai people we saw were dressed in traditional, red-checked cloth and extra-large ear piercings. As we arrived in the village (a goring of houses arranged in a circle), the men lined up and performed Adumu—the jumping dance—where they competed to see who could jump highest. This energetic dance is typically performed at weddings and religious and cultural events, but also for the curious Western tourists!

The Maasai are one of the most iconic tribal groups across Africa and the one I remember studying with deep curiosity in elementary school. They are a nomadic, warrior tribe, and surprisingly, they still retain many of their traditions as if the outside world doesn't exist.

Most interesting was speaking with a woman named Cora who worked at the camp but was also from that village. All of the Kauffman Fellows asked her question after question about what it was like growing up there and how she was able to leave, because in that part of Africa, most women don't.

As challenging as it is being a woman in VC, we all agreed that it was nothing compared with Cora's journey, and it was a continued lesson in how many people, especially women, find ways to grow and thrive even in the confines of what, to us, felt like somewhat restrictive traditions and cultures.

It made me think about safety in general—both of the emotional variety (how Cora had somehow tapped into the gumption and emotional "courage" to leave her village for different opportunities) and the physical.

Africa is a vast and complicated continent (housing a whopping fifty-four countries), with countless cultures and communities—and competing interests. When you're in Nairobi, Kenya's capital, you feel incredibly safe and able to go anywhere, but each time we entered our hotel, we went through a metal detector and had to have our bags screened. That was a reality check for sure. Kenya has an unfortunate issue with terrorism from neighboring countries looking to destabilize the country and dissuade tourism. Nairobi is where many foreign workers across Africa actually live, so it's an interesting tension of feeling very at home with all the cultures living there, while also being a bit of a target (the Westgate Mall attack in 2013 is the one people usually think about, in which seventy-one innocent people were killed).

Not only did I hear about the terrorism concerns from several locals but many were also transparent about the reality of poverty. Once, while in a taxi, the driver made a point of driving us by Kibera, the largest slum in Africa, where the average person earns around $2.00 per day.

What I witnessed was heartbreaking and made my stomach churn—people living on top of one another, piles of garbage everywhere, and children without shoes, or really anything at all. Ultimately, being a person who travels means being made aware of both the magnificence of different parts of the world—the expansiveness of humanity, at times—and also the bleakness.

I wondered if that's why so many African entrepreneurs are what I describe as "empaths," solving problems they experienced firsthand with a corresponding reflective (and sometimes even emotional) tint to them. Of course, you can also find these types of founders in the US, but there's been a noticeable shift toward founders there looking for white spaces and what I call "opportunistic entrepreneurship." I have invested into both of these types of founders in my portfolio, but as a former founder myself (and one who considers myself in the style of the empath), I relished witnessing and talking with Africa's deep bench of empath founders on my Kenyan trip.

After the Summit, *TechCrunch* covered my thoughts in this area, along with my overall perception of Africa's startup and venture capital scene:

> We have invested in Africa for the last few years.... Each time I come to the continent, I discover founders thinking bigger and even more globally-minded than the last time I visited. The first few times I came here, I heard a lot about scaling across the country, then the continent, and now founders talk about dominating the globe. That mindset is really exciting for a fund called Everywhere.

My trip to Africa was, in and of itself, a macro experience: zooming out and gaining a big picture perspective. To invest in African technology companies, one needs to have a macro view of the future opportunity—which is not perfectly obvious. While the opportunities are vast, the associated risks are real. Even as more venture capital dollars flow into Africa at the early stage, it's always a question of where these founders will secure their next round of capital in order to scale. But if you really believe, as I do, that the next Google and PayPal and Amazon will be built on the continent, then you need to buckle up, appreciate the risks, and take the long view that the market will continue to evolve.

Being MACRO, as it shows up here, encapsulates having a worldview that is broader and deeper than the average person's. It's about taking in the whole panorama of humanity—the very good, the very upsetting, and everything in between—learning from all of it, and using everything as the bricks to build your own unique path.

MACRO IN ACTION:

 » *Zoom out.* The Maasai is a relatively small, tribal group, but their ability to maintain their unique and proprietary culture without compromise is nothing short of extraordinary in this fast-paced world. Seemingly small things can have an outsized impact—it's only a matter of perspective.

 » *Think long-term.* The startup world in Africa has been rapidly developing, but many investors are still wary of leaning in based on the challenges and risks associated with investing there. It's easy to shy away from the region because of these challenges, but taking a long-term view puts the massive opportunity into focus: long-term investors will get the upside of investing in this time of early growth, which presents more risk but also more potential return. Overall, I tend to believe more is to be gained by taking a longer-term, more macro view. When I was in Kenya, for example, I learned that their president and governors have big plans for the country, but they don't talk in two-to-five-year time horizons; rather, they are looking ahead and building for ten to fifty years into the future!

» ***Think global, act local.*** I originally had no idea that I could access and invest successfully into African-based companies while living in NYC. Five years later, I have a portfolio of a dozen startups from the region and a better sense of the strategy needed to build a global portfolio. We never could have started investing in the region without trusted people on the ground (founders and investors) working closely with us. And why would the best founders in Africa want to take investment from a small venture fund based in NYC? Well, to gain access to our global network, which can help them as they think about scaling globally, raising capital, and attracting talent.

BABS OGUNDEYI, CO-FOUNDER OF KUDA

When he told me that the name of his company Kuda means "love" in the Shona language, it boded well for my conversation with Babs Ogundeyi, Kuda's Nigerian-based founder.

My excitement about Nigerian startups was a slow burn over years rather than a sudden epiphany. When I heard about many of the challenges they faced, it put all the stereotypical Stanford tech bros to shame. They weren't just dealing with the ordinary startup hand-wringing around finding product/market fit, but rather things like currency fluctuations, corruption, and a venture capital world generally unfriendly to the existential risk of doing business in a place like Nigeria.

These founders needed to be *tough*, and Babs was certainly that, though his calm presence and demeanor sometimes hid that inner warrior.

Since 2019, when Babs created Kuda as an online "challenger bank," it has made what can only be described as significant strides. By 2024, it had reached nearly $60 billion in transaction volume and had amassed seven million retail and business customers—not a small accomplishment for a relatively new startup.

On my trip to Kenya for the Kauffman Summit, as I mentioned earlier, I met with quite a few consumer fintech startups from across the region. I heard reference to Kuda bank time and again: "We're the Kuda bank of Kenya" or "We're the Kuda bank of Ghana" were common refrains.

On that trip, I'd planned to head next to Lagos to meet with investors and founders, but the world had other plans for me. My visa was tied up, and I'd caught a nasty stomach bug while on safari, so I reluctantly headed back to NYC to recover but was eager to meet up with Babs, whom I'd heard so much about during my trip.

When we finally sat down for our conversation for *Venture Everywhere*, Babs began by telling me about being raised in London in the earliest part of his life but then moving back to Nigeria with his parents, where he felt more at home in the truest sense (in part, of course, because he *is* Nigerian). But then he returned to England to attend boarding school, where he excelled at sports like rugby, hockey, and cricket (and also excelled at playing the piano—yet another founder I profile in this book who is an artist in some way!).

With that experience, especially with his entrenchment in athletics, Babs told me, "I came into my own. I was now confident."

Babs's mom's entire family, including his grandmother, was very entrepreneurial; in fact, his mom was a well-known and very successful wholesale merchant in Nigeria, so his entrepreneurial roots were well-laid. And, his burgeoning self-esteem helped guide him toward his first entrepreneurial impetus, which was throwing and promoting parties (for "a little change" in his pocket, he told me).

But the lure of Wall Street was too tempting, temporarily steering him back away from the startup world. "I planned to be the Wolf of Wall Street—pinstripe suits and red Ferraris," Babs laughed. "I thought, *Yep, that's the life for me*—so I studied business and accounting to go into investment banking."

After graduating, he stayed in England to follow that path, interning at an investment bank, which ended up changing his perspective rather severely. "After that," he said, "I just knew that I could never work in an investment bank. It wasn't great."

To shake things up, he went on to work at Pricewaterhouse-Coopers, where, although all of his clients were banks, he got to work with a lot of companies and witness different dynamics and ways of doing business (which later informed his approach as an entrepreneur).

While in that role, he felt compelled to move back to Nigeria, but he continued to toggle back and forth between Nigeria and his adopted home of England, as well as lots of other places that his work at PwC took him to.

This part of our conversation was interesting to me. Going back and forth between two places, both of which feel like home, requires a certain amount of shape-shifting, with Babs having to adopt different personas for distinct locations—I'm no stranger to this phenomenon, having experienced it myself when I've lived in different locales.

He likened this to what he gained from his sports-oriented school years: he'd travel to different locations to tournaments and away games, adapting (not to mention being productive on the field or court at the same time) from a young age. This became a roadmap for his big-picture, cosmopolitan thinking as an adult and entrepreneur. It was all part of his Everywhere Mindset.

ᕼᕼ

While working his full-time job at PwC, Babs also became a founder in two different side hustle startups. One was a recruiting company called EazyCareers (which, he told me with a laugh, "Was fun, but failed."), then a business with his cousin called Mototrader, a centralized marketplace for second-hand cars.

The failure of Careers taught him that, while a great idea was one thing, brand awareness and distribution almost eclipses that in importance, so, for the second company, they focused squarely on that strategy as a centerpiece, enlisting newspaper vendors (individuals selling newspapers on the street after buying them in bulk) as partners by paying them a small fee to put the printed *Mototrader* magazine inside their stash of papers.

As fate would have it, the owner of one of the newspaper companies was reading the paper, came across the *Mototrader* magazine, and ended up becoming the buyer of their company.

That first exit bolstered his confidence, but Babs didn't actually start Kuda until after he'd left PwC and worked for a stint in the Nigerian government, where he was a special advisor on finance in one of the Nigerian states. This gave him an entirely new set of insights and skill sets. "The public sector is a lot different [than the private sector]," he explained. "You have to be more streetwise. You have to understand people more. You have to find a balance between trust—or the perception of trust—and all other kinds of nuances."

Inspired by yet another new perspective, Babs came to realize that there was a better way to offer financial services to the masses. "It had to be affordable, had to be accessible. I was used to Africa always getting substandard products that people tried and rejected," he said, before he continued with determination in his voice, "So I wanted a product that was made by Africans, built by Africans, but that was on par with, or even surpassed, other global products."

Babs forged ahead, buying an existing small bank (the fastest way for them to go to market) and changing the name to Kuda before they'd even completed the transfer of ownership. With that, the risks piled on. "I'd sold my house to be able to buy the bank and get the banking license we needed," he told me.

As I mentioned earlier, I've learned a lot about how difficult doing business in Nigeria can be, and on top of that, I admired Babs's ability to continue to raise the bar on his personal risk barometer.

"I just had great conviction, and I knew that if I didn't believe, there was no way anyone else would believe, so I had to," he said, adding with a laugh, "Because, although today it doesn't sound so crazy, at the time it was quite ridiculous—a faceless bank, no branches. *Okay, good luck.*"

Then, he continued, "I will have to 'back' myself. This is a bank. It's regulated; it's people's money. It's got so many moving parts that you have to be really on top of it. And you can't come out with a semblance of a bank. You are either it or you're not."

Like I observed from the get-go, Babs comes across as fearless, very "in it to win it" like the athlete he was growing up. But he also has a really calm core, which I see as unique and one of the key factors in his ability to wade through a really challenging industry in a really challenging environment and country, all the way to success.

"There's so much chaos in entrepreneurship, especially fast-growth, regulated stakeholder management. For me, it's the ability to just remain calm and eye the prize," he said. "It's never as bad as you think it is, and even when it's good, it's never as good as the media make it out to be. There's a certain relentlessness with that because it allows you to just stay on course, whatever the case, either high or low. And you need that calmness to get through every situation…because there's always a situation."

One of those situations was when he was shopping for groceries in a supermarket, and he happened to notice that the person in front of him in line was about to use a Kuda bank card. He said when he saw it, "All I was thinking in my head was, *Oh, my gosh, I hope it works.* And it worked, and I was so relieved and excited. And then, of course, I brought out my card as well. And the cashier asked, 'Is this a foreign card?' And I said, 'No, it's a Nigerian card.' Then she said, 'Oh, do you work there?' I said, 'Well, you could say that.'"

We laughed together over that cute exchange, and Babs told me that having a huge vision—and his own belief in it— then seeing it work in the real world was "almost like a drug."

In that sense, then, there's a counterbalance to Babs's typical coolheadedness—because, he told me, when you're building something vital to the world, there's also "always something to get excited about," whether it's something relatively small like the first few customers or something huge like an injection of millions of dollars of venture capital into the business. "To become the biggest thing you can," he said, "you just have to take lots of little steps, one after the other."

Those measured steps—and a myopic focus on the prize—is also what keeps Babs from being pulled in a thousand different directions amidst the multitude of Kuda's milestones and goals. "You have to be very strong, because as you grow, your stakeholders increase," he noted. "And there's no formula—you develop your strategies as you go along based on the experiences that you have, assessing the situation on a daily basis."

Then, he said, it becomes a different kind of pressure when investors are involved, along with some potential conflict sprinkled in. "Different investors with their different strategies want you to do different things," he told me, adding with a smile, "And they all believe that their strategy is the right one."

I've, of course, seen this firsthand, sitting on boards where each investor had a very different vision and strategy for the company. That can be stressful for founders who are pulled in different directions. It doesn't help that most VCs have strong opinions strongly held—including me! But ultimately, I personally am betting on the jockey, not the horse.

Babs continued, "You need to be very strong in your conviction on what to do, and you have to be able to make your own decisions in spite of all these different calls from different places. At times, I've tried to please everybody, but you can't do that. You can't please everybody. Certainly, [you] can't please everybody equally. And this thing about pleasing people, if you don't do it 100 percent, you haven't done it. So you might as well not bother because it's just a waste of time. You need to just do what you believe will work for your business and for you."

In that same vein, Babs gave voice to something that some founders might be reluctant to implement when the need for funding is strong—the ability to say no to potential investors and their money if they're not a fit. He told me a story about an early investor, whom he termed a "devil investor" instead of the typical "angel investor" moniker, who ultimately tried to undermine Babs and the business. A big lesson that not all angels are angelic!

"So, inasmuch as investors conduct due diligence on you as a founder, you absolutely have to DD investors as well," he said, "because you need to see yourself as the magician. You're the one. You need to turn water into wine. You need to be confident enough to say, 'Well, actually, no, I don't want to be in bed with you.' And you can only say that if you do a proper DD, which is one of the things that I [originally] didn't do."

Every founder has to man the ship when all manner of hell breaks loose (devil investors definitely included). Even the calmest of waters get hit by unexpected waves sometimes, and Babs/Kuda was no exception. Like when the COVID pandemic happened simultaneously with a large investor pulling out…after Kuda had started deploying the promised capital.

"I panicked," Babs told me frankly. "Those were the scariest moments."

He went on. "I personally had the ability to keep going because it's not over unless it's actually over. The only option, as far as I'm concerned, is to be positive until there is absolutely nothing to be positive about. Sure, you might have to make a few tweaks here and there. We didn't actually let go of anybody, but we let the whole team know that things were going to be tight, and we weren't going to be able to do some of the things we wanted to do. And that's ok."

"So long as there's still life, anything can happen," Babs told me as we ended our conversation, yet again highlighting his ability to return time and again to his calm center and course correct while keeping his eye on the big picture, big vision, and end goal.

KEY INSIGHTS:
BABS AS A MACRO FOUNDER

» **Be the wolf.** His *Wolf of Wall Street* reference—which seems funny but was his dream and inspiration—is actually incredibly fitting for a macro like Babs. He is highly competitive in nature, in it to win it, and his early sports orientation and travel for tournaments and competing with different teams carved a path to his big picture cosmopolitan thinking later on.

» **Say no.** The most successful (and happy) people have gotten good at saying "No" when it makes sense (and sometimes, even when it doesn't at first). Babs gave the advice that he himself hadn't taken, which was to say no to an investor he knew deep down was wrong for him and his company and with whom he didn't want to do business. Saying no can definitely save lots of problems later, and it also proactively opens the right doors.

» ***Incremental steps for monumental progress.*** Macros always have a strong foundation even when they're future-leaning, and Babs was no different. He always wanted to be the biggest thing he could be in business, and the way to do that was, for him, to take lots of little steps one after the other. Often referred to as the "next right action," this is a simple but effective way to make progress in anything at all: from baby steps to the big leap.

CHAPTER 12

UAE AND SAUDI ARABIA

When I lived in London, many of my friends were from the Middle East—places like the UAE, Oman, and Bahrain, all of which I had very limited exposure to before I moved to the UK and therefore seemed far-flung and exotic to me.

On the bank holiday weekends in the UK, I noticed that these friends would hop on flights back home for a quick visit and some sunshine, the way that New Yorkers head down to Palm Beach in February. I'd often be invited on these trips and had the opportunity to experience them as a local, staying in private homes and enjoying mom-made cuisine. It was always surprising to see where my friends grew up—many of their families lived in extravagant homes and literal palaces, which you'd never know from seeing their low-key flats back in South Kensington in London.

The Emirates were my favorite place for a weekend break, because every time I'd land in Dubai or Abu Dhabi, I would barely recognize the place from the previous trip (compare that to London, which feels stuck in time). The development in the UAE has always happened at breakneck speed, and on my early trips there, I saw more buildings and shopping centers being built than startups.

That changed around 2014, when international venture capital firms like Naspers and Tiger started investing into the region, and local sovereign wealth-backed funds like Mubadala and ADQ also started investing into companies, programs, and other VC funds to support the development of the region's ecosystem. Although the entrepreneurial momentum had been building for more than a decade, the rise of mega-successful startups like Souq.com (acquired by Amazon for $580 million in 2017), Careem (acquired by Uber for $3.1 billion in 2020 and whose founder, Mudassir, is profiled later in this chapter), Swvl, and Tabby helped solidify the UAE as a true startup hub.

One of the groups leading the charge was Hub 71 in Abu Dhabi, a platform for all things startup that includes corporates, government, and investors coming together to help founders grow and scale.

In early 2020, they were running a three-month accelerator program in partnership with Techstars, and I spent the day there mentoring the companies in the current cohort and meeting some of the other local investors and corporate partners. It was a treat to interact with so many ambitious founders building companies in some of my favorite verticals (but tailored to the local UAE market). There were healthcare and fintech companies but also agtech, edtech, proptech, and of course, AI companies. What was interesting about Hub 71 is that it welcomed founders from all over the world who wanted access to the UAE market and provided them a friendly landing pad that included subsidies for housing, healthcare, and office space and, most importantly, access to pilots and commercial deals with local companies.

On my most recent trip to Dubai, I had a unique experience unrelated to startups but which was equally thrilling—a torrential rainstorm! I was meeting one of my best friends from LA there for a weekend of fun (she happened to be at a conference in Abu Dhabi that same week). We had booked a luxury hotel on the Palm Islands for maximum "beach" (man-made, of course) time, and while they typically are more likely to get sandstorms than rainstorms, the day we arrived saw some of the heaviest rains and flooding the city had ever seen.

It was clear that our outdoor adventure would have to wait, so our backup plan was to hit the famous Dubai mall. As a born-and-raised New Yorker, any store bigger than the size of a corner bodega market makes me anxious, so I avoid malls like the plague. But on this occasion, I was curious to see the fifty football fields worth of shopping and entertainment options and the impressive shark-filled aquarium that I'd heard so much about. So, I tapped right into my Everywhere Mindset, and off we went. Hours of wandering and fifteen thousand steps later, plus viewing the famous waterfall show and enjoying a great meal, we found our way to the Careem rideshare pickup area in the mall and collapsed in the back seat of the white Lexus that had braved the flooding to deliver us safely back to our hotel.

But I wasn't just in Dubai for a fun-filled weekend with my bestie; I was actually at the tail-end of a bigger work-related trip that started in Saudi Arabia, a place I never thought I would find myself in.

ঙ়ঙ়

Saudi Arabia has recently seen some incredible cultural trans-formations—an official "opening" to the rest of the world. Before my trip there, I could think of nothing other than being able to witness this metamorphosis firsthand in its infancy.

I've always been curious about life in Saudi Arabia. In col-lege, I had a friend who grew up on the American military base there, and she told me countless stories about the polarity of her childhood: on the one hand, she was free to roam the base, eat Kit-Kat candy bars, and attend the American school in her shorts; on the other hand, if she left the base, she needed to be covered head to toe and escorted by a man. But she also had magical stories to share, like riding ATVs across the desert and exploring Al-Ula—an ancient Arabic oasis city—with her class much like US school children visit the Washington Monument in DC.

Since that time, there has been monumental change across Saudi Arabia from a cultural, social, and political standpoint and, most exciting for me, the rise of a vibrant startup community starting to emerge.

In addition to supporting said startup community on their own soil, the Saudi government, as well as family offices there, are investing heavily into innovation globally, taking a unique (and refreshingly long-term) view; the Saudis are not in it to make a quick buck, rather, they're interested in supporting innovation and diversifying their assets across industries and regions. This long-term thinking is a perfect match with venture capital investing, an asset class where returns can take more than a decade to materialize in many cases. Short-term thinkers forget that innovation takes time!

As it became harder for venture capitalists to source capital for their funds in the traditional US enclaves during the tech downturn starting in 2022, many VC funds went to the Middle East—where liquidity is not an issue—to raise capital. In the last couple of years, I've seen countless fund manager friends make the trip to Saudi Arabia and also to places like Abu Dhabi, Dubai, and Qatar.

I didn't go to Saudi Arabia to raise capital, however; I was invited to speak at 2024's LEAP conference, which is the largest tech conference in the Middle East. The organizers made an effort to include international tech people like me on the agenda and enticed me with a prime speaking slot on the main stage in addition to many fun side events. So, I put any reservations I may have had about traveling to Saudi Arabia aside and excitedly jumped on a flight to Riyadh to understand more about the country and its startup scene first-hand.

The first thing I noticed when I landed in Riyadh is just how dry it is—with the city situated inland, it has very little humidity. When I mentioned this to my driver on the way to the hotel from the airport, he remarked that the benefit of such low humidity is that you can dry your laundry outdoors in just two hours.

The second thing I noticed is how modestly everyone dresses, even given that the dress code has been loosened as part of a push to drive a more open society. Men do not wear shorts, and women are covered in varying ways, wearing the full abaya or a head scarf or sometimes just loose-fitting clothing. For my part, I wore modest clothing and a neck scarf (but no head covering), and I felt perfectly fine dressed like that. Going to the gym (separate ones for men and women) was another story. I never quite knew what to wear or if I was inadvertently offending someone, so I settled on wearing a long dress over my Lululemons en route to the gym.

Being in Saudi Arabia is like being at the crossroads of two distinct worlds—one traditional and acutely more foreign and one that feels much more familiar. One evening, we walked into Carbone restaurant in Riyadh, and I was easily transported to their New York City flagship on Thompson Street in the Village or one of their Miami or Las Vegas outposts… minus the alcohol. So, while it felt odd to be sitting down to a decadent steak dinner without an overpriced glass of Barolo wine, I otherwise felt right at home.

[Side note: in place of alcohol, the country seems obsessed with smoothies. Breakfast, lunch, or dinner, it doesn't matter—the Saudi version of this delicious fruit concoction is served up regardless of the time of day, cuisine you are eating, or, for that matter, the venue you're eating it in.]

One evening, a bunch of us were invited to watch a soccer game at the Kingdom Arena (Saudis are *very* into soccer, so the vibe and energy was amazing). We also got to experience Boulevard World, an impressive entertainment complex that felt like Las Vegas on steroids. The area contained replicas of several landmarks from ten countries including a mini-Egyptian Pyramids replica and Lake Lagoon, the largest artificial lake in the world, making it into the Guinness Book of World Records. Everything in the country was bigger!

I didn't see much greenery my entire trip, and it struck me as an analogy for everything Saudi Arabia is trying to do right now; it's so much harder to make things grow there, but they're utterly determined to make that happen.

And the entrepreneurial impetus is in the same vein: the government is investing significant capital into the startup ecosystem and attracting foreign funds and businesses who are willing to have a presence in Saudi Arabia, which can obviously be quite a draw. They're pushing to attract and import every kind of talent and idea and company, versus the way it happens in other countries, which is much more organic. In Saudi Arabia, they're going from zero to one hundred fast, and they have the resources and the drive to do it.

༖༖

I really saw the country's progress on innovation front and center when I arrived at the 2024 LEAP Conference. With 215,000 people attending (yes, you read that number right), it was, by far, the largest annual tech conference in the Middle East.

One interesting thing I learned from one of my Careem drivers that I hadn't realized before my arrival is that more than 40 percent of Saudi Arabia's population are non-citizens, coming instead from Yemen, the Indian subcontinent, and other Arab countries. Many of the Careem drivers are from Yemen, and the hotels tend to be staffed by people from the Philippines, and it was helpful and informative to have those perspectives sprinkled into my purview throughout my trip.

I had a couple different roles at the conference, and the first was speaking about the future of investing in humanity, which was obviously a big topic. It was on the main stage of the conference, and it was a great opportunity for me to evangelize our Everywhere Ventures investment thesis, which is investing in products and people that make the world a better place (in areas like health, finance, and climate, for instance) without wearing the official "impact" investor moniker.

In the middle of an important point during the panel, I looked up and noticed a server walking around and serving coffee (which in Saudi Arabia is a tiny, white porcelain cup filled with a delicious blend of coffees, cardamom, and other spices) to the VIP attendees in the front row, something you would never see at a conference in the US. It was another example of Saudi hospitality right in front of my very eyes.

Aside from speaking at LEAP, I spent my days meeting with local startups and local investors that I might want to co-invest with and some of the other players in the tech ecosystem.

Before I go on any trip, like a good Systematic, I do a lot of pre-work, making sure that I have all the introductions I need, and I make as many meetings happen on the ground as possible. For example, I did a ton of research on the Careem community before I went on the trip. Plus, I set up a LEAP WhatsApp group a few weeks ahead of the event to help coordinate everyone for dinners and events—despite the fact that many of the others were local to the region and I was not.

❖❖

In Saudi Arabia, I was like a fly on the wall, getting a chance to see the country opening up. With more and more opportunities cropping up there as we speak, it will never go back to its infancy again.

Being among the first wave there to witness that growth—and to be a woman doing so—was really cool, because I've seen before how this plays out. When there's such a huge "blue ocean" of opportunity, everyone starts rushing in, and things change quickly. In a few years, Saudi Arabia may very well become another Dubai…or something entirely different.

As I have written in other chapters, a lot of the first generation of founders we've seen in many markets are locals who go off to places like Oxford or MIT, get some training and learn from different paradigms, and then return to their country to make their mark and impact.

In fact, in Saudi Arabia there's an emerging "Careem Mafia," a new generation of operators spinning out of later stage startups (or scale-ups) to start their own companies. I met with a couple of founders there who are alumni of Careem. The startup system is growing organically there—and it's working for them.

I've described this phenomenon before. The ecosystem is only just beginning, then it will mature as founders' experience trickles down and translates into new ventures. In Saudi Arabia, we're watching history being made in real time.

This iteration of SYSTEMATIC in *Venture Everywhere* offers a counter to conventional wisdom about rigid structures (and systems). Just because something is systematic doesn't mean it isn't open to evolution or flexibility. In fact, systems and Systematics are often willing to grow and change, typically based on resources and data and within

more prescribed parameters. **Think of the growth of Saudi Arabia and its Boulevard World—that magnificence, while it might seem magical and visionary, is really only manifestable through systems.**

SYSTEMATIC IN ACTION:

» *Evolve the system.* The great opening of Saudi Arabia is evolving the traditional system into something entirely new, and the change we are seeing has progressed from primary to systematic. There is so much planning and progress, but it's all occurring in a rather organized way, almost like a master plan for the country which follows a particular timetable. As I point out, from there, Saudi Arabia could evolve into the next UAE or something else entirely. You can be systematic in your approach without knowing exactly what things will look like at the end.

» *Measure twice, cut once.* Planning and preparation, as mentioned a number of times, are the hallmark of the Systematic. This was here evidenced by the huge amount of preparation I undertook before arriving in Saudi Arabia to meet startups and local VCs. I've developed a methodology for entering a new market that works for me, which is to research thoroughly and then partner with locals who are super plugged in.

» *Count your wins, not your losses.* Systematics love data as a signpost for moving forward, but it also helps see reality clearly, understand when things aren't working, and move on when warranted—like when it was pouring in Dubai, and we couldn't have our planned day of exploration so instead went to the mall and had an (unexpectedly) great time.

MUDASSIR SHEIKHA, CO-FOUNDER OF CAREEM

I was at the Kauffman Fellows Global Summit in Dubai in early 2020 when I first heard about the ride share, deliveries, and payments app Careem. Kauffman had given us all a special code for discounted rides across Dubai for the duration of the summit, and I excitedly downloaded the app because the rides were rumored to be faster, cheaper, and more reliable than any other service. Plus, all of my colleagues from the region were already huge fans, having watched over the years as the company went from startup to market leader, then getting acquired by Uber for $3.1 billion a month before I landed in the Middle East on that trip.

My interview with Careem founder Mudassir Sheikha is the "seed" of some interesting new thinking around entrepreneurship in two ways. First, his story will open up a different perspective to people since many of us have no real concept of what life is like in the Middle East, much less starting a business there. Also, as I mentioned earlier in the chapter, Careem as a company is a seed of sorts, single-handedly spawning an entire new generation of founders, which some call the "Careem Effect" or, more colloquially, the "Careem Mafia" (mirroring the so-called "PayPal effect" in Silicon Valley, which showcases the original PayPal founders who all went on to start massive second companies). Over 100 Careem alumni have gone on to become startup founders themselves, raising upwards of $600 million in funding.

❦❦

When I sat down to chat with Mudassir, the first word that came to mind to describe him was "humble."

He was born and raised in a middle-class family in Karachi, Pakistan, and both of his parents were strong influences on him growing up, albeit in different ways. His dad was a shop owner (selling rice and grains), through whom, he said, he saw entrepreneurship and its struggles, but also people doing interesting things, doing it on their own, living flexible lives, and being their own boss.

His mom, who might have been called a "tiger mom" in a later era, Mudassir said, laughing, focused on raising him and his two younger sisters, explaining that since she hadn't gotten a chance to pursue her own education, she ensured that all three of her kids got the best ones possible.

Mudassir left Pakistan for the first time to attend the University of Southern California (USC) as an undergrad. I tried to imagine what it must have been like coming from Pakistan—even from a relatively more diverse city like Karachi—as an eighteen-year-old and landing in Los Angeles, so I asked him about that.

"There was definitely a culture shock in some respects," he said, but it was more the shock of going to a brand-new place without his protective parents and away from what he called his "sheltered" life.

It was the first time he had to look after himself in every way, from doing laundry to cooking to getting a job on the side for living expenses because, he explained, "I didn't want to be a burden on the family. Everything in dollars was a bit out of reach, so it was best if I could just do things on my own and not have to bother them with it. It was growing up quickly and looking after myself—that was a bigger challenge."

With a dual major in economics and computer science, Mudassir graduated in 1999—significant because that year was approaching the height of the dot-com bubble, which would shape his professional life in many ways in coming years.

And while he wasn't yet pulled to entrepreneurship himself, he was inspired by everything that was happening around him. "I looked around and thought, *Wow! A lot of people my age are doing big things, and they don't look very different from me.* And they also came from very humble backgrounds. So, all of a sudden, I started to build some confidence that this is something that I could pursue as well."

He was seriously entertaining two job offers and ended up going with Trilogy Software, which was the lesser-known brand of the two but the one with higher compensation. "The paycheck seemed more interesting," he told me with a smile. Plus, the cost of living in Austin, Texas, where they were headquartered, was low; not to mention, Austin was a great city for a recent college grad.

After a four-month training regimen, the company flew the new employees to Las Vegas, and it was there that Mudassir's more corporate trajectory started to veer off course. While there, he received a phone call from a friend who'd just joined a startup as "employee number one" in Silicon Valley that had just raised $200 million—and the friend convinced Mudassir to join them.

Mudassir and I talked about how, at this time—the halcyon years of 2000—the startup world operated very differently than it does today. It was, he and I agreed, a time of extreme excess, deviating from reality and real company-building, in order to focus on many of the wrong things, like the ability to make millions upon millions and buy private islands and jets…in your twenties.

We all know how the dot-com story plays out: there was what was generously called a "correction" when the dot-com bubble burst, followed quickly by the terrorist attacks in the US on September 11, 2001. That, of course, impacted the startup Mudassir was working at, which quickly found itself underwater. To make matters worse, employees there decided that they should buy all of their equity up front to save on taxes, so he put every dollar he had into buying out his stock options.

Then those went to zero, and he lost everything. "It was, from a financial perspective," he told me, "a disaster."

But as these things go, it was also a huge learning experience. Building to flip (selling quickly to make a quick profit) was the ethos during those early tech-boom years, but as we learned, that is usually unsustainable. Sitting during our conversation from his current vantage point—as the CEO of Careem, which is on a long-term journey, building brick by brick over the last twelve years and counting Mudassir said, "The biggest learning was build to last."

"You don't know what's going to happen around you, so you have to be building the right foundation and be prepared to stay with something for your life," Mudassir told me. "And if you do that, then the decisions that come out of it will help you get the right outcomes. So always build to last."

The second biggest learning? Speed. Or perhaps better said, slowing down. Because, Mudassir explained, "Building impactful companies takes time." And it doesn't have to include sleeping bags in the office and incessant twenty-hour workdays.

After all the tumult in Silicon Valley, he said, it was time to move back to Pakistan—in part, to look after his parents, and also to finally consider a company of his own, seeing opportunity in the dearth of infrastructure around the consumer finance boom occurring in the country at the time.

The problem was twofold. Mudassir himself didn't have the capacity (financially), nor, he said, "the appetite," to really take that on, especially because the building blocks in the country just weren't there to pave the way for entrepreneurs. From there, Mudassir's professional path wound yet again (not unlike so many other founders), and he stopped off in 2008 to take a job at esteemed consulting firm McKinsey, where he spent four years in the Dubai office.

It's interesting to hear Mudassir's experience around that juncture because it was so similar to my own path. He faced a true fork in the road where he could have gone either way—perhaps starting his own company was hard from a financial standpoint, but he had all the learnings under his belt. Still, he chose a different, more corporate and stable direction.

In many ways, though, McKinsey was a catalyst for him. Most important, it was where he met Magnus Olsson, who later became his co-founder at Careem. Coupled with the Device Anywhere company exit—another startup he's had a stint at—which finally put a cash cushion in his pocket, Mudassir started to feel ready for a bit more risk.

Then something even more pivotal happened. Magnus had a near-death experience (a brain aneurysm), and when he came out of surgery, a survivor, both men had an epiphany regarding what life is about. For them, it was, in part, about finding a huge idea and running with it.

That was the genesis of their company, yes, but also said Mudassir, "To build something big and, more importantly, something meaningful. That has a legacy on the planet." He added, "There was a view that we can do it, we have to just give it a shot. And if we give it a shot, there's a good chance that we will get there."

The clarity was contagious, not to mention mutually beneficial, and both men forged ahead with Careem from that moment on.

But, of course, as the story often goes, the happy ending was still out of reach, and they were, said Mudassir, naive as to just how difficult it would be. As he and I had discussed earlier, there wasn't much of a local startup ecosystem at the time, and such environments are vital for support, resources, and, of course, funding.

And if the fundraising ecosystem was difficult, the talent ecosystem was even harder. People from the region at the time wanted to work at more stable and high-paying multinationals, not a startup, and in general weren't prepared to risk working for equity instead of cash, which to them wasn't a logical move.

Careem faced a third layer of challenge—they had to build the *foundation* they were going to build the *company* on. Google Maps wasn't yet accurate or reliable, so they had to build their own maps and point-of-interest database; many people in the region did not have credit cards, so they had to build their own cash collection systems; and they had to build a communication infrastructure.

"All of these things that you take for granted when you're building something in the US or Europe were just not there," Mudassir noted.

And then there was the doubt—and in many cases pushback—that they faced from friends and former colleagues. *So many founders experience this, but the commonality doesn't take away the sting of being underestimated, and I'm always impressed when people can find the wherewithal to keep going in spite of it.*

They did this, said Mudassir, by going back time and again to their dual drivers of seeing growth and making an impact. "We were seeing more and more customers using the product," he said. "We were learning things; we were developing things. And you could see that there's something here. You could feel it in your gut that something is here."

Mudassir continued, a big smile blooming on his face when he told me, "And then, this is one of the beautiful things of the ride sharing business, you see impact every day, multiple times a day. Every time you get in the car with the captain [driver], he tells you his life story and what impact you're making in his life and his family's life. It's so incredibly energizing."

Mudassir visibly lit up when talking about this, describing how, in the early days, those captains would not just be anonymous people; they were part of the team. Every evening when they were done working, they would come to the office, and the entire Careem crew would hang out, the captains reporting what happened during their day, where the competition was coming from, and telling them what was working and what wasn't.

"The impact was so visible and so hard to dismiss that it just was very gratifying," he told me.

I had my own moment(s) of joy with my Careem driver in Saudi Arabia, a wonderful man named Saleh, who, by the end of our (very long—thanks again, Saudi traffic!) ride was my own personal tour guide and new friend.

🐦🐦

With all the founders I interviewed for *Venture Everywhere*, I like to delve into leadership, because I'm always intrigued by how people on such disparate journeys and with unique experiences can evolve into great leaders (or not so great in other cases, but luckily none in this book!), so I asked Mudassir how he was able to tease out that skill as an entrepreneur—distinct from how it would evolve in a corporate setting—something I myself also had to learn along the way.

Mudassir definitely agreed that leadership within a startup mindset ("Move fast and break things," he laughed) was, at first, about *un*learning the consultant mindset. Working hard was obviously not a problem, so, he said, the main thing was to prioritize making decisions quickly, even when you don't have all of the data, reasoning, or research behind them.

"And the rest?" he shrugged. "You just learn."

In the beginning of Mudassir's profile, I mentioned the astonishing reach of the so-called "Careem Mafia." When speaking with former employees of Careem who went on to found startups, there was a unifying message: the company had been an incredible training ground, and, by all accounts, Mudassir was an amazing leader. Oftentimes, when looking at other successful startups, that isn't necessarily the case, or, at least, strong leadership isn't at the tip of everyone's tongues. There seemed to be something really different and very special about the Careem culture and about Mudassir and his team.

"I cannot take the credit because I think the purpose of Careem is a gift," he told me simply, again embodying not only humility but the mission-forward impetus of his company.

It seemed he had a masterful way of communicating that vision in order to attract talent, not just with cash, but with purpose. This is a fantastic example of bringing Systematic virtues to life in an inspirational way.

Mudassir said, "The start of Careem is special, done to create a legacy to begin with—this was the main driver from the start. And we communicated this to people. We were not able to pay market wages at first, so the only people that we were able to attract in the early days were the people that came for Careem's purpose: simplifying lives and building an awesome organization that inspires."

And this purpose, for Mudassir and Careem, is everything—going from grassroots to a booming business in a structured way, but also by, as he told me, "To uplift the region, to give back."

KEY INSIGHTS:
MUDASSIR AS A SYSTEMATIC FOUNDER

» **Build to last.** Mudassir was "lucky" in the sense that he was mired in the dot-com bubble (and subsequent implosion) and learned something really important from it, which is that anything easy and fast is a mirage. Creating a legacy means building something meaningful over time, not looking for or expecting the fast flip or win. It's paramount to figure out how to create longevity.

» ***Reboot the system.*** To become a successful founder, Mudassir had to unlearn the McKinsey way (basically, perfection before action) and instead needed to move more quickly and prioritize making decisions, even when he didn't necessarily have all of the data, reasoning, or research behind them. Rigidity obviously doesn't leave room for flexibility nor mistakes, both of which are needed to build something truly great.

» ***Apply first principles.*** In its infancy, Careem faced the extra challenge of needing to build the foundation they were going to build the company on, so they dug very deep (literally and figuratively) and built their own maps, cash collection systems, and communication infrastructure. Break down complicated problems into the basic components, and then reassemble them from the ground up.

CHAPTER 13

IMMIGRANT FOUNDERS IN THE US

Although my own family has been in the US since the 1890s, we never exactly lost that immigrant hunger and drive to make a better life.

My grandfather—whom I described in the introduction—worked all hours running his fruit stores and, for whatever reason, two generations later, I also share that professional hunger.

I also touched a bit on my own startup journey. Back in the day, I had a roommate from Denmark whose boyfriend Mikael (who'd followed her from Denmark) often hung around our apartment. He couldn't get a proper job since he was in the US without a work permit, so we would talk about innovation and tech trends from time to time. Being from a Nordic country, he knew a lot about mobile technology, in particular, since, at the time, the region had pioneered breakout companies like Nokia and Ericsson.

Mikael had a highly technical friend from school who was *also* living in NYC and *also* unable to work legally, so we all started meeting up at night and on weekends jamming on ideas. As it turns out, we had a shared vision but one that arose from different points of view. They were visitors living in NYC and needed to call home frequently and I, on the other hand, had a boyfriend living in Germany whom I wanted to call a lot. Same issue, two sides of the coin. So, we decided to team up to pursue creating the world we wanted to see exist, which meant making affordable international calls on our mobile phones, something that was not possible at the time. I wish I could say I followed an informed startup playbook—one that included intently studying customer pain points, posing the hard questions to my future co-founders (like, for example, what would happen if one of us wanted to leave the company or change roles), and properly researching our market opportunity—but that would not be the truth. Instead, like many empath founders, I dove right in with my heart, determined to solve a problem I knew needed to be fixed.

The company, Switch-Mobile, which we touted as a mobile phone application to make international communication more efficient, convenient, and affordable, had its ups and downs. We did manage to get to product/market fit pretty quickly, but our ability to scale was hampered by our own inexperience and lack of a defensible technology moat.

This is all to say we made a ton of mistakes along the way.

But we did get one thing right, and that was our perfect timing. I learned over the next fifteen years of building and investing into startups that one should never underestimate what an important determinant that is for both good and bad company outcomes. In our case, the iPhone had recently launched, which meant that, for the first time, people had a supercomputer in their pocket—and they needed things to do with it! That's where we came in, at just the right juncture.

Then one day, I took a flight to the famed Consumer Electronics Show (or CES) in Las Vegas where my business partners and I were meeting with some of the bigger players in the telecommunication industry. I ended up getting the last seat on an oversold flight, in the last row near the bathrooms (joy!) without the ability to recline. But the guy sitting next to me was also on route to CES, and he, too, was grumpy about the last row situation. So, we distracted each other by diving into our work, which really meant him grilling me the entire flight about our company, go-to-market, and business model.

Upon landing, he looked at me and said, "I'm going to buy your company." He grabbed his bag, tossed his business card my way, and made a quick exit out the back door of the airplane. When I recounted the story to my co-founders, we all shared a good laugh, thinking it was a pipe dream or a joke.

But it was airplane-man (and his pre-paid payment processor company) who got the last laugh when, three months later, the M&A (mergers and acquisitions) transaction closed, and we had been acquired by his company. Just another reminder from the universe that luck and timing—and even awful airplane seats, which for better or worse, are a part of the Everywhere Mindset—play a huge part in the startup journey.

After going through the merger, we spent a year in "golden handcuffs," the lock-up period where a founder is asked (or required in our case) to work for the acquiring company in order to receive the full value of the acquisition terms.

In my case, there wasn't much to do, but I tried to make myself useful, helping with a few more acquisitions and random projects in Europe. My favorite one was when the CEO asked me to go to Nice, France, to evaluate a data center there. With very poor French, I spent the first week there a bit uncomfortable with the situation but then realized, *hey, I'm being paid to be in Nice, so I may as well live it up!* One week turned into five because, as I told the CEO when he called to check in on my progress, there was a *lot* of due diligence that needed to be done.

After I was personally privy to the complete startup cycle (from inspiration to acquisition), I was never going back. Technology and startups were now in my blood, and it was clear I was going to pursue this path for the long term, and I found that the ideas kept flowing.

Instead of seeing something broken in the world and complaining about it, everywhere I looked there was opportunity for improvement, and that felt like walking around with rose-colored glasses—or opportunity goggles—on. As such, my second company was more planned and opportunistic. I saw a market gap and a clear path to filling it.

This company was in the text message marketing space, but unfortunately, this go-round, that all-important but sometimes elusive timing was off. The company was venture-backed and, for a few moments at least, a darling of the tech scene. But as it happens, the market was not ready for this type of solution (yet—we've come to see a few companies, which started a few years later, do really well in this space… hello, timing!), and I had to shut that company down. At the time, it was a big blow to my ego, especially since I had experienced earlier success, but looking back, that failure makes me a better investor and mentor to founders.

As someone who is self-aware, I always knew that I was just an okay founder. Some of the long list of mistakes I made include: not being a great manager, not being able to compromise, not being strategic enough to scale, not being diplomatic enough to keep quiet…. I could go on. The good part of being self-aware is that I see my skill gaps clearly, but I also know when a skill is a superpower. When I wrote my first angel check and started working with inception-stage founders, I felt that I'd finally landed in my zone of genius. Being an early-stage investor was *it* for me.

I can trace this path backward, back past Everywhere Ventures and past my role at Techstars. In earlier chapters, I've described my journey into corporate venture capital and how I was working on my third company when I took the role as head of digital ventures at the BBC through a serendipitous meeting, but what I learned there was something I knew in my bones: cash is a commodity, and although startups need it, the real value any early-stage investor can provide transcends capital into meaningful support. While the BBC role was amazing because I got to make direct investments and foster incubation and spin-outs, I tapped into my life's work when I founded Labs, the corporate accelerator where we surrounded startups with community and resources and customer opportunities to help them grow.

From my experience running Labs, I was completely sold on the cohort-based, accelerator model, and I wanted to lean into the mentor-focused methodology it utilized. So, I started mentoring founders in other accelerator programs, like Seedcamp in London and Techstars in NYC, which is how I ended up there as the managing director after my time at the BBC wrapped up.

Moving back to NYC full time was perfectly synchronized with the next wave of the tech scene there. While I was running my own company, the startup scene was rather dismal (there was no longstanding startup culture, hardly any founders who came before putting angel money and knowledge back into the ecosystem, and no mentor culture), but by 2014, the venture capitalists had discovered NYC. Founders were flocking to the city, making it a natural innovation hub. There was more diversity than in Silicon Valley, fostering a more international contingent in NYC, which is a crossroads of the world. There were also government programs cropping up to support startups, and lots of new verticals started to thrive there based on the history of industry in the city (think manufacturing sparking the hard tech movement and Wall Street as a precursor to fintech).

Working at Techstars was nothing short of monumental for me. Reviewing thousands of applications per year and interviewing hundreds of founders is a thrill, and it was also amazing training for an aspiring investor like me with the high-volume investment cadence and founder pattern recognition. I learned enough there to fill about five graduate school curricula: I ran eight accelerator programs, invested in a company that went public as well as a couple of unicorns, made some of the closest friends of my life in the other MDs, and I learned a ton about what it really takes to support founders and how to manage a large portfolio by tapping into a larger network.

Being the first believer in someone else's life work is an incredible privilege, and that's the place where I have made (and will continue to make) the greatest impact. And it's not just being an investor, per se, but rather helping other founders not make the same mistakes I made and helping to point them in the right direction. Techstars set me up for my long-term future in a sustainable way.

But at the end of the day, it was still a job, and I didn't always agree with some of the decisions made and our positioning (which is natural at any job). So, I started formulating my own thesis for a fund, using much of what I'd experienced as a founder, corporate VC, angel investor, and head of an accelerator, into a new community-based fund model. At first, Techstars gave their blessing to allow me to run this fund on the side, but as our brand grew, that became uncomfortable for everyone. It was time to make a move.

As I thought about leaving Techstars, I wanted to do something I'd never done in my life, which was really sit down and figure out what was next for me. Yes, my next venture fund was already in the works as a side project, but I wondered every day if it was the right path for me. So, I did something unexpected and set to work evaluating all of my options and running a proper job search.

I interviewed with half a dozen larger funds to be a general partner. I interviewed with a public tech company to run an internal incubation-type division. I even looked at a high-profile role in government. The offers came, but nothing felt quite right.

After going back and forth for a few months, mulling my options, speaking with my closest mentors, and looking within, I realized I was an entrepreneur at heart. Working at a company or building someone else's dream was not going to be fulfilling to me. Despite the challenges of running a micro-VC fund, it's what I'm meant to do…and what I was finally *ready* to do.

I called my business partner, Scott, who, after working with me for four years, wasn't surprised by this turn of events. We rebranded to Everywhere Ventures—a name we felt represented who we were and what we stood for—and then went out to raise the capital for our new fund. The only issue was, because I had taken so long to be struck by my a-ha moment, the market had turned. It was now 2022, and tech had ground to a halt. Another reminder that timing is everything…and right then, it sucked for us!

But we got scrappy. Dusting off that Everywhere Mindset, we decided that if it was hard to raise capital in the US at that moment, we'd figure out another way. We jumped on a plane to Europe, called everyone we knew to help us, and sat down for, on average, six hour-long meetings with potential LPs every day. We were breathless and running on fumes, but it was worth it when, a couple months later, we exceeded our fundraising goal and officially launched our new fund.

Our thesis for Everywhere Ventures is very much rooted in the belief that innovation is everywhere, and investors should proactively seek out interesting founders (globally) rather than sitting on their laurels in Silicon Valley waiting for founders to come to them. This is especially true now because the best founder won't necessarily even be in Silicon Valley anymore.

This global lens is why, in this final chapter, I'm shining the spotlight on a special breed of founders: immigrant founders in the US, who strongly demonstrate Everywhere Mindset attributes and who are thriving because they know a secret about the world that many Americans don't yet know or embrace.

I myself have also experienced being an immigrant of sorts, having lived in several countries over the last twenty years. And though I do business all over the world, part of me still always feels a bit like an outsider wherever I go.

For example, while raising capital for my last fund, I found myself pitching some prominent LPs in Spain. But what was awkward to me, in the room of eight men, was that they mostly talked over me and avoided looking directly at me, preferring to banter with each other as they debated our fund strategy. I left this particular meeting deflated, proclaiming that I would never take money from these antiquated dudes. But the next day, they phoned me, telling me that the meeting went swimmingly well, and they wanted to invest in my fund. From that I learned that, while I might not understand a given culture as an outsider, as an investor (and as a founder) you just have to go with the flow—and I look for that, well, Everywhere.

Over the years, as I invested into hundreds of companies and interacted with thousands of founders, I started to notice patterns and throughlines across some of the most successful ones. As I've gotten to know many of these founders, I've started to focus in on and distill the characteristics and qualities I observed down to a core framework that informed the Everywhere Mindset concept.

The successful founders profiled in this book demonstrate how they've each embraced and cultivated it—usually out of necessity. I have similarly shown how they influenced my own journey from lawyer to founder to investor and the path to ultimately finding my life's work as an early-stage investor and startup coach.

And when I've looked across my portfolio, lo and behold, many of these founders have immigrated to other countries.

৯৬

More than half of the most valuable startups in America were founded by immigrants: Google, Tesla, Stripe, Intel, Palantir, WhatsApp, and others, were all started by people who came to the United States to forge a better life for themselves and their families.

But what is it about immigrants that make them uniquely suited to startup life?

I would argue their diverse cultural backgrounds bring a wealth of perspectives, experiences, and skills to the table, fostering creativity and out-of-the-box thinking, which is crucial for innovation. Consensus-based thinking may be sufficient for a successful career at IBM, but to truly change the world, you need big, bold ideas that require against-the-grain thinking.

Let's not forget the challenges and hurdles faced during the immigration process to this country. I know about this firsthand, having written dozens of letters of recommendation on behalf of my portfolio founders who have applied for the O-1 visa (and yes, they all possess "extraordinary abilities" as required by US immigration services). This type of resilience and elasticity is highly valuable in the fast-paced and unpredictable world of technology startups.

Immigrants often possess a global mindset (or the iteration I've come up with, an Everywhere Mindset), allowing them to navigate international markets, build diverse networks, and identify emerging opportunities across borders.

Additionally, the risk-taking nature of immigration, leaving behind familiar environments to pursue new opportunities, primes immigrants for entrepreneurial ventures where uncertainty and risk are inherent. The ability to persevere through adversity, coupled with a relentless drive to succeed, propels many immigrants to the forefront of innovation and business leadership in the tech sector.

Sometimes, these immigrant entrepreneurs have to deal with discrimination in their newly adopted home, which is on top of the hardships of running an early-stage company.

Furthermore, access to education and talent networks in their home countries or through international connections can provide immigrants with unique advantages, such as access to specialized skills, market insights, and potential partnerships that contribute to their success as tech entrepreneurs.

As I see it, immigrants are the backbone of America, and nowhere is that more evident than in the startup world.

These founders are in America, in part, because the world is getting smaller, and geographies are becoming less relevant—globalization is bringing us all together—and also because the US is still the most developed (and desirable) training ground for founders that currently exists.

వ్యౖ

The data speaks the truth: a 2012 study highlighted in *Harvard Business Review* found that immigrants were more likely to start businesses than members of the native population in most of the sixty-nine countries surveyed. In the United States, where 13.7 percent of the population is foreign-born, immigrants represent 20.2 percent of the self-employed workforce and 25 percent of startup founders. And, according to a 2018 study by the National Foundation for

American Policy, immigrants founded or co-founded 55 percent of the unicorns in the United States.

The article goes on to say that, from a policy perspective, the findings suggest the entrepreneurial potential of immigrants extends beyond the small group of late-stage international entrepreneurs who are usually the target of entrepreneurship visa programs and investment promotion agencies. Per capita, immigrants are about 80 percent more likely to start a company, compared to US-born citizens. "The findings suggest that immigrants act more as 'job creators' than 'job takers' and that non-US-born founders play outsized roles in US high-growth entrepreneurship," the author said.

Other research backs up the idea that immigrants might be more attuned to entrepreneurship. The combination of a drive for success along with a desire to create a better future for themselves and their family is powerful and is often fueled by a strong work ethic.

Additionally, research from the Vienna University of Economics and Business explores the element of self-selection: when people voluntarily choose to emigrate, they're engaging in what many would regard as a risky endeavor due to the unfamiliarity of their new home and the chances of success there. The decisions to emigrate voluntarily and to start a company are both associated with high levels of risk.

As so many of the profiles in *Venture Everywhere* have suggested, a high-risk profile and being Elastic is certainly a commonality among very successful founders. But the Everywhere Mindset also includes an additional five characteristics behind great (immigrant) entrepreneurs—being Systematic, having Moxie, being kinetic, thinking macro, and having Conviction. These all show up in so many different ways in *Venture Everywhere*, demonstrating how commingled—and cultivable—they are in some of the world's most successful founders.

The reason these founders are so successful and tend to be one step ahead of US-born founders, is because they've had to embrace the Everywhere Mindset much earlier on. It's something similar to what I've seen when, for example, New Yorkers move to other cities and crush it. They typically work long hours with high intensity and are more focused and less lifestyle-oriented than many locals, so they outpace them.

The US is a country of immigrants, and it retains that scrappy attitude and bias towards "yes." It is also diverse in culture and thinking, all of which has been shown to produce more successful and sustainable business models. The two founders in this chapter embody that multidimensionality and demonstrate why the US leads in innovation, no matter where people hail from originally.

ᘐᘗ

The best startup pitch decks, which are a virtual representation of a business plan, conclude with a slide titled "Why Now?" This slide asks why *this* is the perfect moment for *this* startup to exist based on a confluence of factors like new technology, economic conditions, societal shifts, and other tailwinds.

It's my favorite slide in any pitch deck because, while most ideas are not entirely novel, it's the execution of the idea, team composition, and market timing that makes them ripe (or not) for success. I now think of my life, each day, as the "Why Now?" slide, and I weigh my decisions against this framework. And you should too; now may be *your* time to follow your passion, start something new, and create the world you want to see exist.

GABRIELA ISTURIZ, CO-FOUNDER OF EBILLINGHUB AND BELLEFIELD

Gaby Isturiz, founder of eBillingHub and Bellefield, is one of those people who is akin to human Teflon. She's been through a lot on her way to success (not least was growing up in Venezuela, which had its own set of societal and economic challenges, and then making her way to the US to work before she even spoke much English), but because of her conviction—and her full embrace of being an underdog at every turn—she seems to conquer every challenge with the ease of Tiger Woods hitting a golf ball. In other words, she makes it look easy.

I originally met Gaby through some Pittsburgh-area founders when we were looking to do more deals in the region. She offered to be our eyes and ears on the ground in that area, which is ripe with startups coming out of Carnegie Mellon University. She also liked our Everywhere Ventures "by founders for founders" model, so she became one of our fund's limited partners.

As I got to know her, I was struck by what a unique talent she was, so in 2021, I convinced her to help me start XX, our sub-fund investing into female founders.

From the jump, Gaby had a strong—and feminist—influence in her mom, who, she told me, instilled in her the non-negotiables of education and financial independence.

From her dad, she received her entrepreneurial inspiration—he was a founder during the Venezuelan oil boom in the 1970s—and tapped into it starting in early childhood, when, for example, she created different styles of hair bows to bring to school and sell.

Interestingly enough, like me and a few founders I've profiled in this book, Gaby was also an artist (painting and sculpture), and her mom encouraged her to sell her artwork, which she also did at school.

"I was always selling!" she laughed. This would serve her well later as a founder.

First, though, in the interest of making a real living—and because her father made her eschew art for a more solid career choice (he told her he was not going to help support her starting immediately upon graduation)—Gaby decided to focus on computer engineering. She told me she chose this field because it had the most balanced ratio of men and women, unlike other fields, which were more male-dominated.

Gaby told me she was "super competitive" and "super ambitious" (I could relate) and moved up the ranks from programmer to management at the central bank in Venezuela. She was still very young and making great money at the time, but her ambition outdid even that—she wanted more—and she planned to find that for herself in the US.

I personally find it amazing that Gaby had the confidence to leave her home, family, and community, not to mention a lucrative and stable job, to come to live the proverbial American dream without speaking any English. It is, to say the least, a road less traveled.

When I asked her what sparked that next level of ambition, she told me, "It was a little bit of ignorance—I didn't know how little I knew—but I think the ignorance helped me."

She went on to tell me a story about getting some job offers in the US, one of which she unknowingly accepted (she thought she'd declined because she didn't understand English well enough to turn it down!). Things were certainly clarified when she didn't show up for her first day of work.

From there, Gaby said, "I worked really hard. I needed to put in double effort to do the job well and to understand the demands."

And simply fitting into the brand-new culture had its own demands and challenges. Gaby is a really funny person, but given the language barrier and cultural differences, she told me that, at first, "I didn't even know how to be funny. And when I was trying to be funny, nobody would laugh."

༽༽

Gaby's founder fate was sealed when two things happened in Pittsburgh: she met her now-husband and co-founder Dani, and around the same time, was hired as the CIO of a large law firm, where she got hired to solve a problem building in-house software.

In the first inkling of her later journey as a founder, she also saw a different problem, and an idea for solving it sparked, but it would require building something completely outside of her experience: commercial software to allow for ease in logging attorneys' billable hours, bringing the very first software as a service (SaaS) concept to law firms.

She pitched it to Dani with the caveat that she couldn't leave her job as CIO because the money was too good. Dani, too, was making good money but offered to leave his job to build the first prototype.

Gaby then had the genius idea to ask her boss if they could deploy their protype at the law firm where she worked to get proof of concept for the commercial project, and he agreed, not quite realizing what a gold mine they were sitting on.

She laughed when she told me that he said, with a figurative condescending pat on the head, "'We're going to allocate a little bit of money for this little project of yours, and you guys do it, but please don't leave us.' They didn't take me seriously."

Gaby and Dani forged ahead without venture funding, and Dani handled all the coding and sales at the beginning. For her part, Gaby was working full-time at the law firm on top of building the company. She also got a consulting job to make up for the income that Dani was not bringing in and, in quick succession, had two babies. It took three years of this for eBillingHub to bootstrap their way to their first million dollars in revenue, and when that happened, Gaby finally quit her job at the law firm to become full-time CEO.

It's not uncommon to hear this kind of story from women entrepreneurs—women are really good at "doing it all" but often get incredibly burnt out and sometimes fall on their faces. But Gaby once again proved her uniqueness. In her case, she did it all, but also *had* it all, reveling in every second of that crazy, rocky journey.

"I loved it so much. It never felt like it was working, and we wore all the hats," she said with a fond smile. "It was exhausting, but it didn't feel like that, because that was just our life. And it was a family affair. The kids were running around, and we needed to master product, we needed to master sales, we needed to master marketing. And be good at all that. So, we got pretty good at it."

Even with that, Gaby told me, there were times she wanted to give up and settle back into stability and a steady (and sizable) paycheck in corporate America like she'd done before.

What kept her going in the startup world? In large part, her symbiotic relationship with Dani. He framed their professional choice as a slam dunk, and she tapped into their foundation of deep trust to believe him.

Though Gaby and Dani are not the only married co-founder team in this book (see Chapter 2), I still had to ask how they managed to work together, live together, and maintain a solid (and loving!) relationship.

Gaby laughed again as she told me, "It's been a journey, because you have two Latin individuals. And we're both very loud and very passionate about our points of view."

She continued, "But, we always agreed on what was best for the company. And we also agreed to never let any differences in the company impact the family." Then she added, "As I got more sophisticated as a CEO and as a founder, I put together a framework for conflict resolution, and I wrote it down and reviewed and updated it constantly. So, when we couldn't agree, we went back to the framework."

In my many years in venture, I've seen lots of co-founders' relationships, some good and some not so good, and I think this is solid advice for anyone in that position, especially co-founders facing communications challenges or conflict. Gaby and Dani don't communicate verbally because it doesn't work well for them, so they found another way, which is writing things down.

Over the years, I have also gotten to know Dani too (they're adorably inseparable). In fact, Dani was in the room while I was interviewing Gaby on Zoom for *Venture Everywhere*, and he messaged me after the interview, saying, "Our framework to resolve disagreements is really succinct. Rule Number One: Do as Gaby says. And it works!"

꙰꙰

The eBillingHub story was filled with lessons and had a David versus Goliath-style ending. They were approached by Thomson Reuters (a behemoth in the media and information space) to do a partnership, which seemed like a dream come true.

"I talked to their CTO," Gaby told me, "and gave them all the inside info about our product, because I was so excited that we'd closed a partnership. Then they announced their own [competing] invoicing product."

That news was devastating to Gaby, but Dani convinced her it was an opportunity, saying, "If they're copying us, we're already a threat. But they cannot do this better. We've got this, we just need to beat them."

"So, we started eating away at their market," Gaby told me. They did all of that successfully, and soon after, Thomson Reuters came back to them with a partnership offer, and eventually, an acquisition offer. They weren't quite ready to sell, but they had a devious—or devilish, as we've seen with other founders like Babs in Chapter 10—angel investor on the capitalization table who made things very difficult for them, so they decided to do so.

The exit was substantial, but after nine years of building their company, they also felt regrets about selling. This is a common theme with founders, even when the exit is good.

But very quickly, Gaby (and Dani) bounced back and started a new company, called Bellefield, this time creating the first mobile time-tracking software for lawyers, using entirely their own capital. They sold that to a public company, Roper Technologies, in 2020.

Gaby might have been somewhat of an underdog in her early life, but for her, that became a true position of power and a launching pad, catapulting both her resilience and her appetite for risk.

"Growing up in Venezuela," she said, "You have a survival instinct for everything. We developed that early on, but we also had the knowledge and the work ethic to really build something big."

In another part of our conversation, Gaby revealed something else about being underestimated that I thought was really interesting. "It didn't bother me," she said. "It gave me a little bit more space and more wiggle room for failure. There is nothing wrong with being the second best."

I realized there's something about this that adds to her cachet as an investor too. So often VCs look for the obvious wins, but Gaby is really good at sussing out the "diamond in the rough" and, over our years working together, I've watched her blossom from a founder and operator into a great investor. She's slow to warm to a deal, but once she does her own work and soul searching and builds up her conviction, she very quickly goes from calm and cool to passionate and (loudly) determined to invest.

"When I get there, I really get there. Conviction is something that I also mastered through practice, like curiosity and learning. It's always getting out of my comfort zone—like with a muscle. It's the deliberate practice," she said, a serious glint in her eye, adding, "No bullshit on this end, Jenny."

Muscles are, by their very nature, elastic, shifting shape with time and circumstance (and through wear and tear). Earlier, I compared Gaby to Tiger Woods, and over the course of our discussion, I realized that likening her to a pro athlete was a pretty apt comparison. She's been "training" for the founder's life all along.

KEY INSIGHTS:
GABY AS AN ELASTIC FOUNDER

» ***Know when to let go.*** Elastics bounce back easily, but they also know when to change course. In Gaby's case, when the option to sell her company was on the table, it was an incredibly tough decision for her. She even felt as if it was something they were pressured into by an opinionated investor, but ultimately, she knew it was the right move.

» ***Things are more similar than they might seem.*** Gaby (like me and a few other founders in *Venture Everywhere*) has a strongly artistic side to her, which she eschewed in order to follow another path into computer science. At first glance, the two might not seem to have anything to do with one another, but the

Elastic persona like Gaby is adept at borrowing skills and transferring them from one area to another to bolster the overall approach and forward movement.
» *Experience isn't always everything.* When Gaby had the idea for her company, she needed to step outside her comfort zone of professional experience and build commercial software, something she had never done. She did it, learning along the way, and perhaps even benefited from seeing things with a beginner's eye.

JONATHAN LEVIN, CO-FOUNDER OF CHAINALYSIS

In another life, if he wasn't a crypto entrepreneur, I think Jonathan Levin (whom I refer to here as Jony), the founder of Chainalysis, would have been a guru or spiritual guide of some sort; it seems to be part of his DNA to see the future and have a vision that will change the world.

On a more micro level, Jony's parents left South Africa with a literal Everywhere Mindset in tow, seeking a better life for their family and, as Jony described, "settled at the first port that they went to," which was London.

His parents knew nothing about the UK, had no family there, and no real knowledge about how any of the systems there worked. When we chatted about this part of his upbringing, he referenced another influence he thought contributed to both his familial impetus toward moving forward as well as his own path to building a company, and that's the history of the South African Jewish community. In that, he said, the entrepreneurial spirit runs deep. When Jewish people arrived in South Africa at the turn of the twentieth century, many of them built businesses that became an important part of the fabric of the country. For Jony, that backdrop offered exposure and inspiration, especially as his family continued to spend time in South Africa even after moving away.

I first met Jony and his co-founder when they were considering applying to my Techstars program in the US after founding Chainalysis a few months prior. While his co-founder, Michael, was older and more seasoned (he was also co-founder of one of the early crypto exchanges called Kraken), Jony must have been all of twenty-three years old at the time. But even then, he had an uncanny ability to say *very* bold things, though in a way that got people super excited and ready to buy in.

That would serve him incredibly well in bringing his audacious vision of building the leading blockchain analytics company, which offers compliance and investigation software to analyze the blockchain public ledger (which is used to track the movement of digital currencies like Bitcoin). In other words, they essentially help banks and governments track down the bad actors transacting in crypto.

By the time we spoke for *Venture Everywhere*, I'd known Jony for quite some time, and I'd seen along the way how he faced the roadblocks—which inevitably came with being ahead of his time—with total equanimity. How was he able to do that?

At least in part, he told me, it stemmed from being a competitive athlete and playing sports. "I was definitely motivated by the challenges that were always in front of me," he said. "If there was any type of competition, I liked to compete in it."

Competition also applied to his academic career, and he used his required research project during his postgraduate time at Oxford University as a litmus test for cryptocurrency; students get points for rigor and technical prowess, and they also get big points for independence and innovation. Fascinated by the tech behind crypto, Jony studied it like a science and ended up getting one of the highest marks in class under the rubric of "unique contribution to the literature."

By age twenty-two, Jony had become a self-taught expert in the new and still very unknown arena of cryptocurrency, seeing the bigger picture before he had even embarked on his entrepreneurial journey in earnest. "That put me in a position I'd never been in. [When] I walked into every room, I knew more about the subject than anyone else," he said. "And that opened up an opportunity."

A commonality of so many successful founders I've seen, some of whom I've described in this book, is that they tend to seize those opportunities, especially ones that are a little more off the beaten or more traditional path. When Jony was a grad student, he caught what he calls the "lucky break" of talking his way into a consulting role with executives at Western Union. He took that on and conducted a major research project for them, which contributed to the (long) view that he would start and execute something big himself.

He'd built enough confidence—especially through athletics—to forge forward to a nearly indestructible degree, but another compelling component of Jony's macro mentality is centered in his micro-level understanding of human nature (his own included). An avid cyclist, he knows how to use different gears to get where he wants to go, but he first gauges where he's at in the moment. In the same way, regardless of the long term, he told me that an important skill for entrepreneurs to have is the ability to tap into different sides of their character.

"It's very difficult to have all of those parts of your character present at all times," Jony said. "I think the emotional intelligence that you need is to know when to use which of those gears and when to be in real listening mode with true empathy for the people around you and really trying to understand what are they going through. Then, you need to flip to, 'it's my way or the highway'—when seventy-five investors are telling you your startup is never going to work."

"The job of this crazy journey is to know at what points you try and engage those parts of your character the most," he concluded. "And I think the most successful entrepreneurs really get to flex all of those different parts of their personality at different points in the journey. I try to identify which type of moment it is."

Speaking of his love of cycling (not to mention determining what to do in a given moment), Jony used to show up at the Techstars office every day on his bike (he lived in Brooklyn and the office was in Manhattan's Flatiron district) and often walked around the office in bike shorts. One time, a person from the bank he was trying to close a deal with unexpectedly showed up at the office. Without a hitch, Jony ducked out the back stairs onto 23rd Street and into the nearby Levi's store to grab a pair of pants. He was young and somewhat irreverent, but he knew that bike shorts were not going to close deals with people who worked in corporate security. As he ran by my desk, I grabbed him to cut the tags off his pants, then he sprinted back to the conference room to make the meeting.

We laugh about that now, but it tracks with what I said in the beginning, which is that Jony just gets human nature, and in our conversation, I saw even more clearly how much his vision in business is tied to authentic relationships and connections.

He told me about being at a conference in New York and listening really closely as the CEO of MongoDB spoke on a panel and articulated his business strategy more clearly than anything he'd ever heard. As soon as the panel was over, Jony chased him down the street to get his email and ended up connecting with him (and they're still acquaintances all these years later).

"People often forget that humans relate the most to authentic people rather than business leaders in particular," he told me. "So, an important part of me succeeding as a leader is understanding how to cultivate that and how to use that effectively."

Then he added with a laugh, "And a British accent in New York also helps. It gives you at least a few advantages."

৯৬

Jony and I are especially aligned when it comes to learning about both business and the overall human experience through travel, and his Everywhere Mindset plays into his vision of the future: interconnectedness is, after all, baked into the name of his company!

Chainalysis's strategy relies on international expansion—this was a forced direction from the beginning in a way that most businesses aren't forced, because crypto is a global market, and there wasn't a big enough market in the US to solely support the business in the early days. Figuring out how to land in a market and develop it has been one of the company's central strengths.

"My interest when I'm traveling the world is meeting local people and understanding the shared experiences that exist in all of those different places," Jony said. "There are such similar parts to our human experience that allow you to relate to them much more easily when they crop up in your business."

This important component of their business circles back to their strategy around international expansion. Jony told me he's most proud of the fact that when Chainalysis opens in a new market, they tend to feel very local, in the sense that their local offices have their own understanding of how things should work, but they also adopt some of the global Chainalysis best practices, all in order to come together to build.

"That's been something that people get confused about if they don't have a global mindset - how to execute it well," he said. "But if you go to our Korean office, you would think that it's a Korean company that copied Chainalysis, which is how it should be."

That showed me once again how, in his trajectory, the micro contributes to the big picture, and the hinge is, quite literally, flexibility—the need for it is wide and deep in a high-growth startup. Yes, there are many similarities among us as humans, but at the same time, there are nuances in how we conduct ourselves, culturally or otherwise, which also translate to business.

Being amenable to things like doing deals in a sauna in Finland or over a meal ritual in Japan, Jony said, prepares you for the many stages your company will go through.

⇜⇝

Ultimately, I wanted to get to the heart of how Jony balances his huge, future-leaning vision and worldview with the day-to-day realities of running a high growth startup.

First, he said, "What ends up being the thing that gets you through the ups and downs has to be a gut-level, real intuition that you're building something magical."

Then, it must be something you think will really happen in the world one day—it's lofty—but also grounded in some sort of longer-term reality. "You should always be able to go back to that with comfort," Jony said. "That it's something that *will* happen."

Next, you have to get buy-in from stakeholders (something Jony is really good at).

Finally, he said, you make incremental progress toward the future you want to see exist.

"The thing about the day-to-day and what you need to execute, I find that to be a very different part of my brain, where I think about what we need to achieve in six months in order to hit our next milestone," Jony shared with me, adding that, on the other hand, "the company vision should not be something that you're measuring in six-month increments; it should be something that's bigger and more dreamy."

Jony talked about another issue he and a lot of founders face: the hard part is that the vision relies so heavily on factors outside of their control. "We were selling our product and slowly gaining market share, but we couldn't figure out how that actually tracked to our vision," he said. "And in the early days, investors were having a really hard time seeing the vision too. Part of it was our fault as we didn't craft a good narrative around how the minuscule monthly revenue was tied into a much grander vision."

It's a complex ecosystem and journey, and Jony's macro moniker comes full circle when, toward the end of our conversation, he told me point-blank that he recognizes this is a ten-year-plus journey, and he finds peace and sanity in simply knowing that. This is in stark contrast to many founders and business leaders focused on that quick win.

While Jony is a big thinker with a huge vision and our debates can skew to the philosophical at times, he also has a playful side which I imagine has kept him going all these years into building Chainalysis.

At the Techstars demo day back in 2015, after describing a future world where decentralization and transacting anonymously is the norm to an audience of hundreds of investors, he ended the presentation showing the classic meme of a dog sitting behind a computer keyboard typing, "On the Internet nobody knows you're a dog."—a nod to his British humor and recognition that not everything should be taken so seriously.

KEY INSIGHTS:
JONY AS A MACRO FOUNDER

» *Travel widely.* The overall takeaway of *Venture Everywhere* is, of course, joy in, and the benefits of, travel. I loved how Jony described it: traveling widely really allows you to see and understand (to some degree) disparate types and groups of people, which opens up whole new worlds in your own life. Travel also influences your day-to-day business decisions, as it did with Chainalysis's decision to locally brand each outpost of their company in different locations.

» *Mix it up.* As Jony described, you have to work on something you believe will actually come to fruition. macros like him are masters of blending a big vision but grounding it in reality.

» *Find your tribe.* Among the biggest obstacles (and opportunities) for any big thinker is that you are often light years ahead of everyone else and are often met with resistance when others don't see the future as clearly. Jony built his credibility by first honing his thesis around crypto in an academic setting, a place that is typically more open and supportive of new concepts and ideas. This also allowed him to develop his confidence and gain allies and superfans before he shared it with the rest of the world. Finding his early believers and the forward thinkers within his community gave him the necessary support and knowledge (and cheerleading!) to later not only start a category-defining company but also to take it to the next level.

ACKNOWLEDGMENTS

This book wouldn't exist without the unwavering support and encouragement of many people throughout my life. It all started with a spark – a desire to share the incredible stories of those who dared to dream and build something extraordinary. That spark was fanned into a flame by the entrepreneurs who bravely opened their hearts and shared their journeys. Your stories, filled with candidness, vulnerability, and unwavering passion, are the lifeblood of this book. Thank you for entrusting me with your truths and for allowing me to witness and share your resilience.

This journey wasn't a solo one. I'm deeply grateful for the unwavering support of the people and communities who helped me get here, especially my past and present co-founders, colleagues and friends from Fieldston, Columbia, JPM, BBC, Techstars, Kauffman Fellows, and everyone in the Everywhere Ventures family. You've all, in your own ways, contributed to this book's creation.

A huge thank you to my writing coach, who patiently guided me through this process, and to the team at Post Hill Press for believing in this project.

ABOUT THE AUTHOR

Jenny Fielding is a seasoned venture capitalist and technology trailblazer with a diverse background in law, finance, and entrepreneurship. As the founder of two tech startups, she understands the challenges of building companies from the ground up. Now, with a decade of investing experience and a portfolio valued at $10 billion, Jenny leads Everywhere Ventures, the go-to venture fund for early-stage founders around the world. Beyond investing, Jenny is an adjunct professor at Columbia University and Cornell Tech, where she inspires the next generation of entrepreneurs. A sought-after speaker, Jenny has been featured on Bloomberg TV, the *Wall Street Journal*, *Forbes*, and *TechCrunch*, among many others.